THE LIFE OF SERVANTHOOD

THE LIFE OF SERVANTHOOD

Discipleship in the Pattern of Jesus

TIMOTHY C. TENNENT

Copyright 2023 by Timothy C. Tennent

All rights reserved. No part of this publication may be reproduced, stored in a retrieval system, or transmitted, in any form or by any means—electronic, mechanical, photocopying, recording, or otherwise—without prior written permission, except for brief quotations in critical reviews or articles.

Scripture quotations are from the ESV® Bible (The Holy Bible, English Standard Version®), copyright © 2001 by Crossway, a publishing ministry of Good News Publishers. Used by permission. All rights reserved.

Scripture quotations marked NIV are taken from the Holy Bible, New International Version®, NIV® Copyright © 1973, 1978, 1984, 2011 by Biblica, Inc.™ Used by permission of Zondervan. All rights reserved worldwide. www.zondervan.com. The "NIV" and "New International Version" are trademarks registered in the United States Patent and Trademark Office by Biblica, Inc.™ All rights reserved worldwide.

Printed in the United States of America

Page design and layout by PerfecType, Nashville, Tennessee

Tennent, Timothy C.
   The life of servanthood : discipleship in the pattern of Jesus / Timothy C. Tennent. – Franklin, Tennessee : Seedbed Publishing, ©2023.

   pages ; cm.

   ISBN: 9798888000137 (paperback)
   ISBN: 9798888000113 (epub)
   ISBN: 9798888000120 (pdf)
   OCLC: 9798888000137

   1. Jesus Christ--Servanthood. 2. Service (Theology) 3. Servant leadership 4. Discipling (Christianity) 5. Christian life--Methodist authors. I. Title.

BT738.4.T46 2023   266/.023   2023944157

SEEDBED PUBLISHING
Franklin, Tennessee
seedbed.com

To the memory of Howard Grant Myers (1927–2023),
whose faithful life and dedication to his family
modeled the life of servanthood.

Contents

1. God's Servant Brings Justice to the Nations 1
   Isaiah 42:1–9; Matthew 12:15–21

2. God's Servant Brings Salvation to the Nations 17
   Isaiah 49:1–6; Psalm 87

3. A Servant Body You Have Prepared for Me 31
   Psalm 40; Hebrews 10:5–12

4. The Two Songs of Servanthood 43
   1 Samuel 2:1–10; Luke 1:26–38, 46–55

5. Servanthood in the "Other" Parable
   of the Two Sons. 57
   Matthew 21:28–32, 33–46; 22:1–14; Luke 15:11–32

6. Servanthood in the Storm 71
   Psalm 89

Contents

7. Christ as Suffering Servant 85
   Isaiah 50:1–9; 52:13–53:12

8. Servanthood in an Upside-Down Kingdom 99
   Matthew 20:20–28

9. A Lesson in Servanthood: A Lion, a King,
   and a Dead Prophet 113
   1 Kings 13

Epilogue 129

— Chapter One —

God's Servant Brings Justice to the Nations

Isaiah 42:1–9; Matthew 12:15–21

The theme of this book is servanthood. For most Christians, the very mention of the word *servanthood* sends us quickly into reflecting on how we can position ourselves and our future ministries to better serve a world that is broken and desperately in need. Broadly speaking, that is a good instinct to have. However, I do not think it is the best starting place as we begin to think about servanthood. Indeed, if we go too quickly to the fruits of servanthood—namely, all the things we ought to be doing to serve others—without being grounded properly in the roots of servanthood—the theological foundation of servanthood—we will diminish the scope, depth, and cost of what God is calling us to. Without close attention to the roots of servanthood in a distinctly Christian vision, our work will be diminished by at least two difficulties.

First, we will find it difficult to articulate what makes the church different or unique from organizations like Save the Children, March of Dimes, Oxfam, the European Anti-Poverty Network, or any other secular organization that is also committed to serving those in need. It is somewhat like asking what the difference is between counseling and Christian counseling. Is there some qualitative contribution that is uniquely Christian in how serving others is understood or framed or executed?

Second, we will have a hard time understanding the particular role and voice of the church in servanthood alongside a huge array of Christian organizations committed to servanthood like World Relief, World Vision, Habitat for Humanity, and so forth. Even today, more than 90 percent of humanitarian organizations are faith-based, not secular. So, how do we relate to these amazing and effective organizations? After all, Habit for Humanity is a lot better at building houses for the poor than almost any local church would be. World Relief or Bread for the World are a lot better at working with a refugee crisis halfway around the world than almost any local church would be. So, is our role as the church to merely support these effective Christian organizations? Is there a distinctive voice of the church in expressing and embodying servanthood that is theologically anchored and biblically compelling? I believe there is.

To fully explore the theological roots of servanthood, we are going to begin with the Old Testament. The New Testament provides a road map to help Christians understand how we relate to the Old Testament and, obviously, one of the great themes in the New Testament is how Christ fulfills the Old Testament. But the New Testament also develops a surprising theme that was often overlooked in the messianic expectations from the Old Testament; namely, Christ as Servant. Or, to put it even more pointedly, Christ as Suffering Servant. We are accustomed to hearing how Christ is the great Prophet, Priest, and King (Acts 7:37–38; Heb. 4:14–16; Rev. 19:16), but we also need to understand that he is also the great Servant, and the fulfillment of the great call to servanthood, every bit as much as he is the fulfillment of the priesthood or sacrificial system. Indeed, the servanthood of Christ is the theological foundation and root of a biblically grounded understanding of servanthood.

The Servant Songs of Isaiah

There are four messianic passages in Isaiah that have been widely identified as a distinct collection of texts because they highlight a "Servant of Yahweh." The word *Yahweh* is the revealed name of God in the Old Testament. Out of respect for this name, almost all modern translations of the Bible avoid using the word *Yahweh*, but instead, use the word *Lord* in all caps. It is important that you know the word *Yahweh*, because this is not just the general word for "God" or "Lord." It is the revealed personal name for God, derived from the revelation of "I AM WHO I AM" in Exodus 3:13–14.[1]

These four poetical passages in Isaiah are called the Servant of Yahweh Songs, or the Servant Songs. These four texts are found in Isaiah 42:1–9; 49:1–6; 50:1–9; and 52:13–53:12. This chapter will focus on the first Servant Song found in Isaiah 42:1–9. The four songs as a whole are linked together with four prominent themes. First, the Servant is sent on a mission from Yahweh. Second, the mission involves vicarious suffering (i.e., suffering on behalf of another). Third, although the Servant will suffer

---

1. The four sacred consonants YHWH are vocalized by inserting the vowels for the Hebrew word for "Lord," resulting in Yahweh or Jehovah.

and be rejected, he will, in the end, be exalted and vindicated. Finally, his suffering will bring justice, salvation, and blessing to all nations. These four Servant Songs are clearly messianic because the New Testament, as well as the early church, makes the connection to Jesus. Various strands of the Servant Songs are quoted by Matthew, Luke, Paul, Peter, Clement, and Justin Martyr, among others.

In the opening verse of this song (Isa. 42:1a), the theme of servanthood is introduced. Yahweh's messenger is called his "servant" and his "chosen," who is the delight of the Lord: "Behold my servant, whom I uphold, my chosen, in whom my soul delights." In the previous chapter, God recalls his covenant with Abraham and his calling forth Israel as his redeemed people. Twice he calls Israel his servant: "But you, Israel, my servant" (Isa. 41:8) and again in verse 9, speaking to Israel: "You are my servant." Even though God speaks to Israel in the singular, it was generally understood by Jewish writers that these texts were referring to Israel collectively. The people of God are being referred to as a collective single, the corporate servant of God. This is why, even up to the time of Christ, these texts from Isaiah about the Servant were not generally understood as messianic, since they had been recognized as applying to the nation as a whole.

In Isaiah 42, the Servant is particularized and spoken of in more personal, intimate ways which clearly moves us, at least potentially, into the realm of a messianic hope. But it continued to be used as an analogy for the nation as a whole all the way to the time of Christ's coming. In fact, there is one place in the New Testament where Israel is referred to as the servant of God, and that is found in Mary's Magnificat: "He has helped his servant Israel, in remembrance of his mercy" (Luke 1:54).

The New Testament writers who were living in the sunrise of Christ's revelation make the transition and begin to connect these songs to Jesus as specific, individual-focused messianic passages fulfilled in Jesus Christ. They did this not only because of what they were witnessing in Jesus Christ, but, frankly, because Israel had so clearly failed in their mission to embody the servant motif. In the New Testament, the Messiah uniquely embodies what it means to be a Servant of the LORD. This movement from Israel, as the national embodiment of the Servant, to Jesus Christ as the one true Israelite is extremely important in preparing us for what actually unfolds in the life and ministry of Jesus of Nazareth.

The New Testament recognized that in the coming of Jesus Christ, we encounter one who, in a singular way, truly embodies servanthood and what it means to be the Servant of God alone. The first example of this in found in Matthew's Gospel where the song from Isaiah 42 is quoted in length and applied directly to Jesus (Matt. 12:18–21). Thus, Jesus as the true, final Servant of God begins to flourish in the preaching of the early church. Jesus fulfills the servanthood theme, which was a kind of messianic surprise that extended the fulfillment of the Old Testament beyond the expected messianic themes.

The early sermons of Peter continue to develop this surprising theme. After Peter heals the man crippled from birth in Acts 3, he refers to Jesus, saying, "the God of our fathers, has glorified his servant Jesus" (v. 13 NIV). Later in the same sermon he drives home the global, Gentile mission when he declares: "And in your offspring [referring to Abraham and his descendants] shall all the families of the earth be blessed. God, having raised up his servant, sent him to you first, to bless you by turning every one of you from your wickedness" (vv. 25b–26). Later in chapter 4 after Peter and John are released from prison and go back to the gathered church, they pray a powerful prayer. Part of that prayer mentions how Herod and Pontius Pilate conspired with the Gentiles and the Jews "against your holy servant Jesus, whom you anointed" (Acts 4:27). Here again is the messianic language of "anointed one" connected to Christ as the Servant of Yahweh. At the end of that prayer, they ask God to stretch out his hand through his church and perform miraculous signs and wonders "through the name of your holy servant Jesus" (v. 30). Paul refers to Jesus as a servant in Romans 15:8 and, even more important, passes on to us the famous kenosis hymn in Philippians 2, one of the earliest Christian hymns in the New Testament: Christ, "who, though he was in the form of God, did not count equality with God a thing to be grasped, but emptied himself, by taking the form of a servant, being born in the likeness of men" (vv. 6–7).

With these passages found in the New Testament, we are moving into a deeper understanding of the incarnation, God coming to dwell among us as a Servant. We have learned to reconcile Christ as both King from the line of Judah and as priest from the line of Levi, but we have not given as much attention to how Christ also brings together the fulfillment of both King and Servant. This is a key insight that will clarify the questions and tensions that I noted at the outset of this chapter.

With this background, let's circle back and look carefully at Matthew 12:15–21, where the Servant of Yahweh from Isaiah is referenced by Matthew and applied to

Jesus. Matthew has just mentioned how Jesus has been healing the sick and has now withdrawn to a quiet place and instructed his followers to not tell anyone who he is. Matthew says that this is "to fulfill what was spoken by the prophet Isaiah" (v. 17), and quotes the first four of the nine verses of the Servant Song. It is important to note that the selection of these four verses precisely identifies what part of Isaiah's prophecy Jesus is fulfilling. If the focus of fulfillment was on Jesus coming to heal the sick, then Matthew would have quoted the seventh verse of the Servant Song about opening the eyes of the blind or releasing the captives, but he doesn't do that. Instead, he focuses on the earlier part of the song which describes the larger mission of Christ as the Servant of Yahweh. This is important because healing the sick is obviously a vitally important fruit of servanthood, but Matthew draws our attention to the root of servanthood (of which healing is a natural overflow). In other words, he focuses not so much on what Christ *does* as who he *is*, and in the process clarifies that all that he does is an expression of and outflow of his role as Servant.

Let's look more carefully at the mission of the Servant as found in Isaiah 42. There are four major affirmations about the Servant that are highlighted in the text:

1. He will be endowed with the Spirit: "I have put my Spirit upon him . . ." (Isa. 42:1).

Here we have a prophetic picture of the Spirit of God descending upon the Servant of God, setting him apart and empowering him for his mission. You cannot read this as a Christian without thinking of Jesus, the one true Israelite, the Servant of God, standing in the Jordan River with the Spirit of God descending upon him to set him apart and anoint him for his redemptive mission in the world. Matthew recorded that scene in Matthew 3:13–17, and clearly references the Isaiah 42 prophesy.

Looking back from the New Testament, one cannot miss the Trinitarian hint in this text. The Father sends his Servant, which we know from Matthew's Gospel is actually none other than Jesus, the second person of the Trinity. The Father endows him with the Spirit, which we also know from Matthew's Gospel is God the Holy Spirit. We see here, in retrospect, an early hint of the Trinity.

But notice how the Trinity, which is hinted at here and, more important, developed further in Matthew's Gospel, is not the Trinity in the way we often talk about it. We mostly speak of the Trinity as a theological framework for understanding the nature of God as triune. However, the way God actually reveals himself to us in the gospel is connected to his mission. God is redemptively acting in the world. The Father sends the Servant; the Servant heals the sick and proclaims justice; the Spirit anoints and empowers. These are active, missional verbs, not static descriptions of being. God is sending, acting, anointing, preaching, healing, rendering justice, and so forth. This is not Aristotle's "Unmoved Mover." This is God on the move. He is on the move to bless and redeem the world and to set things right. This is in stark contrast to the gods of the Greco-Roman world. Although they believed their gods were powerful, they were also described regularly as passively inactive. Cicero, for example, described the gods as those who "do nothing and care for nothing" and those who "possess limbs but make no use of those limbs."[2] The so-called "god of the philosophers" is not the revelation of God in the Gospels!

This is precisely why, in the Wesleyan understanding, we cannot separate theology from practical theology or the doctrine of God from the mission of God. It is also why we do not separate our servanthood from the Servant of God. There should be no awkward separation between God's person and God's action. Isaiah 42:1 also says that "he will

---

2. Cicero, *De Natura Deorum* 1.51 as quoted in *JETS*, vol. 64, no. 1 (March 2021): 95.

bring forth justice to the nations." God reveals himself and his nature in the context of his redemptive mission in the world. In the same way, we as his servants will reveal him as we serve in the world. For us, there is no servanthood separate or disconnected from God's Servant, Jesus Christ.

Today, we are experiencing a renewed cry for justice in our world. Many very diverse organizations are committed to bringing their understanding of justice to the world. Amnesty International, the ACLU, and the Equal Justice Initiative are examples of organizations that seek to extend justice into the world in ways that may resonate with some aspects of the Christian vision. As Christians, we should be on the forefront of the justice movement, but we should do it in a way that rests solidly on biblical and theological foundations. So, what is our distinctive voice as we join this cry for justice?

First of all, one of our foundational beliefs that eludes the wider society is our affirmation of the image of God that is present in all people. This is the basis of universal dignity. Second, while we appreciate the contextual identities that frame modern understandings of justice, we recognize that the larger group identity of being either "in Adam" or "in Christ" is at the heart of how the biblical vision sees the world. In that sense, justice is directed not only to those who are disenfranchised in an economic or political sense, but to all people who need to hear about the justice of God that comes through the cross of Jesus Christ. Third, the modern framing of justice has been expressed in the context of suspicion, division, and rage, whereas the Christian vision is love, compassion, and extending the shalom of God.

In our text, all the nations of the world are being invited to participate in the salvation and justice that comes through Yahweh's Servant. There is an inherent humility when we realize that Jesus Christ, the Servant of Yahweh, is the only one who truly embodies justice. Therefore, there is no easy separation of acts of justice from the person who fully embodies justice and is on mission from God to bring justice to the nations. We, of course, will be called to join with the mission of Jesus Christ in the world in a wide variety of ways, but we see justice holistically within the framework of the larger redemptive plan of God. This is the power of the Wesleyan message which does not unduly separate justification from the whole redemptive work of God that is at work to sanctify us and to transform society. This is a deeper, fuller, more biblical view of the meaning of the word *salvation*. Matthew uses the language of "[making] disciples of all nations" (Matt. 28:19) not simply to make converts of individuals, but to always understand the larger framework of God's redemptive work, which involves deep personal transformation as well as God's healing of the whole of creation.

2. The Servant of Yahweh extends the reign and rule of God through humility rather than power (Isa. 42:2–3).

The Servant of Yahweh will "not cry aloud or lift up his voice . . . a bruised reed he will not break," and yet, in humility he will "faithfully bring forth justice" (vv. 2–3). This is where the kingdom operates in a way that is unintuitive for the world. In the world all influence and change is extended and understood through power dynamics. Economics, political influence, racial theories, global alliances—everything is interpreted through the lens of power and the extension of power over others vis-à-vis those who lack power. In the early church, the people of God were mostly powerless and disenfranchised, and yet they were God's instruments to bring justice and hope to the world. Today, for the first time in many centuries, the gospel is again being brought to the nations primarily from peoples without power.

3. *This Servant is a light for the nations (Isa. 42:4).*

The Hebrew text of verse 4 says, "the coastlands wait for his law," but the Septuagint (the Greek translation of the Old Testament used by the early Christians) translates the passage as "the nations [or Gentiles] wait in hope." The Greek translation insightfully represents the wider mission and movement of God to send his word to all nations. Using the word for all the Gentile nations (people groups) of the world who are being called to hope points to the Gentile mission as being at the heart of servanthood. Isaiah not only envisions a greater deliverance, but an enlarged covenant with a global reach. Through his Servant, Yahweh will embody and bring "a covenant for the people" because he will be "a light for the [Gentiles] nations" (v. 6).

4. *This Servant* is *the covenant (Isa. 42:6).*

This Gentile mission that was opened in verse 4 is explained further and expanded in verse 6b: "I will give you as a covenant for the people, a light for the nations." The NIV translation says, "I will keep you and will make you to be a covenant for the people and a light for the Gentiles." We often think of Christ as *bringing* a new covenant into the world or *making* a new covenant. However, here Isaiah says that the Servant *is* the Covenant. Jesus embodies the new covenant.

This is why we proclaim Christ into the world. Our servanthood must have a cruciform presence in the world. Our mission cannot be reduced to various things we do, however noble they may be. The world would love for the church to be reduced to just another humanitarian organization. Many sectors of the church have accepted that our voice in bringing hope and justice is merely horizontal and, frankly, indistinguishable from the world's service to the poor, the homeless, or those lacking justice. But we must resist the horizontalization of the church. We cannot allow the world to limit us to horizontal movement in serving a hurting world, with the absence of a vertical message of God's singular inbreaking to establish justice and reconciliation in ways the world can never imagine.

So the great theme of this passage is Jesus Christ, the Servant of God who embodies servanthood. We must see our most basic understanding of servanthood is a call to embody Jesus in the world. All that we do in servanthood flows from the Person who has reconciled all things to himself through sacrificial service to a lost world.

→ Chapter Two ←

God's Servant Brings Salvation to the Nations

Isaiah 49:1–6; Psalm 87

A Scottish nun was there at the consistory where the pope elevated several bishops to the high office of cardinal in the Roman Catholic Church. She couldn't help being a bit patriotic as she was celebrating her Scottish bishop being elevated to such a high office. After all, she was from Ayr, Scotland, the home of Robert Burns, the great bard of Scotland and arguably the heart of Scottish nationalism. In fact, she was quite a sight as she stood there in full habit, waving a small Saint Andrews flag—not the Union Jack, but the Saint Andrews flag. (Saint Andrew is the patron saint of Scotland.)

After the high ceremony she was interviewed by someone from the *Boston Globe* who was there covering the event. When asked about the future of Christianity, she responded: "I'm very worried about the prospects of Christianity. The churches are getting emptier and emptier and there just aren't any young people anymore." Now, this dear nun was speaking from the perspective of someone who was born and raised in Western Europe, the purported heartland of Christianity. Things, from her point of view, looked fairly bleak in Western Europe and, therefore, she concluded that if it is this bad in Western Europe, then the rest of global Christianity must be suffering indeed.

What she was apparently unaware of is that Western Europe (or, for that matter, North America) no longer represents normative Christianity. This is the great new fact of our time. The most important development in the global church in the last fifty years has been the explosive growth of the world Christian movement in the majority world of Asia, Africa, and Latin America. We all know the story of the post-Christian West, but few seem to really understand the emergence of a post–Western Christianity. More people from more diverse people groups with more languages worship Jesus Christ today than at any time in human history. Whether you are looking at linguistics, socioeconomic status, ethnicity, or geography—by every measuring rod, Christianity is the most diverse movement in the world today. The words of Matthew 24:14 are being fulfilled before our very eyes: "And this gospel of the kingdom will be proclaimed throughout the whole world as a testimony to all nations, and then the end will come."

This "great new fact of our time" is not so much a testimony to the plans, efforts, and strategies of the church, but rather to the great initiative of God who made a promise to Abraham to bless all nations. This is a promise that is constantly revisited and renewed through the Old Testament and comes to full flowering in the New Testament. This text in Isaiah, which is the focus of this chapter, is one of the great restatements of this promise.

The second Servant Song is found in Isaiah 49:1–6. This song is explicitly addressed to the nations of the world, reinforcing the point that Yahweh is sovereign over the nations. He declares: "Listen to me, you islands; hear this, you distant nations" (v. 1 NIV). The Servant's mouth has been made "like a sharpened sword" (v. 2 NIV). Through him, Yahweh will display his glory or splendor (v. 3). Throughout the song, the Servant is the speaker, but he only tells the reader what Yahweh has declared. The declaration falls into two separate sections that vividly highlight the particularistic and universalistic strands that are embodied in God's mission through his Servant. Verse 5 focuses on the particularistic mission of the Servant to Israel. He is being sent by Yahweh to "bring Jacob back to him and gather Israel to himself" (NIV). The theme of gathering is central to the Abrahamic covenant, in contrast to the scattering of the nations who stand in opposition to God's sovereignty. Then, in verse 6, as with the first Servant Song, there is a widening of the mission to include the salvation and gathering of the nations of the world:

> he says:
> "It is too small a thing for you to be my servant
>   to restore the tribes of Jacob
>   and bring back those of Israel I have kept.
> I will also make you a light for the Gentiles [to
>   the nations],
>   that my salvation may reach to the ends of the
>   earth." (NIV)

This passage gives a remarkable glimpse into the mission of God. Without diminishing God's mission to Israel, there is an even greater mission that encompasses *all* the nations. Thus, despite the setbacks regarding Israel (rebellion, exile, and judgment), the original promise that

God's Servant Brings Salvation to the Nations

God made to Abraham to bless the nations is still in full view. The unique contribution of Isaiah is the insight that this blessing will be revealed in and through the Servant of Yahweh.

The text begins with an important imperative whereby God addresses, through his Servant, not just his covenantal people, but the distant islands and all the nations of the world: "Listen to me, you islands; hear this, you distant nations" (v. 1 NIV). God is addressing the whole world. Earlier in this great prophecy of Isaiah (chap. 45), Yahweh has already addressed Cyrus, as a reminder that he holds all authority over all the kingdoms of the world. The powerful and arrogant and, frankly, even the fleeting but temporarily powerful kingdom of Babylon must submit to the eternal verities of the kingdom of God. But our text makes it clear that it is not just Babylon that must submit to the eternal plan of God, but all the nations of the world.

The latter part of verses 1 and 2 in our text makes it clear that the voice and manifestation of this authority will not just be through the nation of Israel, but through Yahweh's Servant whom all the nations, even rebellious and exiled Israel, must heed: the Servant of the Lord. His mouth will be like a sharpened sword, implying that he will bring decisive judgment against all who seek to usurp his dominion and his authority and his plans. But it is not the sword of Cyrus which is found here. It is not the sword of the powerful nations of the world. It is the sword of the Word. The Servant of Yahweh will come into the world bearing God's Word, not merely to bring Israel back from its exile and to restore Israel to her earthly promised inheritance—that is too small. Indeed, the greatest exile Israel faced is the exile that is faced by all nations and all peoples, and that is spiritual captivity: "It is too small a thing for you to be my servant to restore the tribes of Jacob and bring back those of Israel I have kept. I will also make you a light for the [nations], that my salvation may reach to the ends of the earth" (49:6 NIV).

The grammatical structure of the text suggests that the Servant of Yahweh is not meant to bring salvation to the ends of the earth, but actually to be "my [Yahweh's] salvation . . . to the ends of the earth." Jesus is more than just the messenger, the herald of this Word. He is the very embodiment of God's salvation for the world. (Paul picks up on this in Galatians 3:16 [NIV] when he says that the Abrahamic promise was to your "seed," not your "seeds"— seed meaning one, not through the instrumentality of the nation, but through the redemption wrought by the Son.) It is not just a message we proclaim, it is the person of Jesus—he is the embodiment of the kingdom. It is this good news that is breaking into the world!

At this point, we need to pause and take note of verse 4. Here, we get a glimpse of what it was like from the Servant's perspective—feeling like his labor was in vain and that his life was spent for nothing. This verse is a reminder that embodying the kingdom into this world was costly and painful for the Servant, and still is for Christ's followers. This theme of suffering and pain, as a central feature of servanthood, will be examined more closely in chapter 7 when we examine the fourth Servant Song. But here we get just a glimpse and then the Servant returns to the purpose for which he was sent.

Isaiah is not introducing something new here in 49:6. This is not a prophetic novelty but a reminder of the original covenant. This far-extending purpose is God winning the nations to himself. This passage from Isaiah is a reminder of Psalm 2, which expands the scope of God's work from Israel to the nations: "Why do the nations rage and the peoples plot in vain? . . . 'I have set my King on Zion, my holy hill. . . . Ask of me, and I will make the nations your heritage, and the ends of the earth your possession'" (vv. 1, 6, 8).

This passage is like the Old Testament version of the Great Commission. That's right, the Great Commission.

This is not the Great Commission as found on the lips of the risen Lord Jesus, but the Great Commission as originally given to Abraham and renewed to Isaac and Jacob: in your seed "all peoples on earth will be blessed" (Gen. 12:3 NIV). This is also the great theme of Psalm 87 that is dedicated to various nations who were the sworn enemies of Israel: Egypt, Babylon, Philistia, Tyre, and Cush. Yet, the nations that they had been taught to hate were declared by Psalm 87 to be fully included in God's plan of redemption. That is why the psalm says that these nations were "born in Zion" (v. 6 NIV). To declare that these nations who had warred against the people of God would be given the same covenantal inheritance as Israel was revolutionary! At one stroke the seven verses of Psalm 87 demolish the widely held notion that the Old Testament is about God only redeeming Israel, rather than his promise to bless all nations through his seed, our Lord Jesus Christ! He is building a house of prayer for all nations under his lordship. This is the global vision you must capture as a servant of God for the world!

Later, when Jesus issues the Great Commission, he is merely extending the promise originally made and now being fulfilled through the preaching of the gospel. You see, ministry can never be reduced to mere tasks the church does; it is first and foremost the mission of God to redeem all nations. Indeed, the last words of Jesus in his earthly ministry recall Isaiah 49:6 when Jesus says, "you will be my witnesses in Jerusalem and in all Judea and Samaria, and to the end of the earth" (Acts 1:8). The phrase of Isaiah 49:6 is found on the lips of Jesus—"that my salvation may reach to the end of the earth."

Later, when the apostle Paul is defending his ministry to the Gentiles, he quotes Isaiah 49:6, but with a very important difference. Remember, Isaiah's prophecy had declared about the Servant of Yahweh, "'I have made you a light for the Gentiles, that you may bring salvation to the ends of the earth'" (Acts 13:47b). Paul does not say this is what the Lord has commanded the Suffering Servant; he says, "For so the Lord has commanded *us*" (v. 47a, italics added). The message Christ embodied is not merely brought by the witnessing church. Paul understands profoundly that the life and witness of the church is an extension of and a fulfillment of this great messianic promise that Jesus fulfilled and then empowered the church to extend. When Jesus says in John's Gospel, "As the Father has sent me, even so I am sending you" (20:21), we realize that the one who was sent into the world has become the great sender into the world.

So don't find yourself thinking too small, or praying too small. God is determined to bring salvation to the ends of the earth. This is about the whole world. This is about the nations coming to our Lord. This is about every knee bowing and every tongue confessing that "Jesus Christ is Lord, to the glory of God the Father" (Phil. 2:10–11)!

This is exactly what began to powerfully unfold from the early church to the present. In the first century, right in the pages of the New Testament, we discover that the gospel was bigger than Judaism as a group of unnamed disciples from Cyprus and Cyrene began to preach the gospel to Greeks, as the text says in Acts 11:20, "telling them the good news about the Lord Jesus" (NIV). The church at Antioch was born, and by the end of the second century became the largest church in the world. It was, you will recall, the sending church of the apostle Paul in his great missionary journeys, which were actually not, as we often think, evangelistic campaigns, but strategic church-planting missions. He was establishing self-supporting, self-propagating, self-governing churches who themselves began to send out missionaries.

By the fourth century this small persecuted sect of Christianity became the official faith of the Roman Empire. The gospel continued to spread north into the so-called Barbarian territories and to the far reaches of the empire itself, including a flourishing church which arose in North Africa and gave wonderful gifts to the church like Saint Augustine. The Eastern Empire, whose capital was then in Constantinople, brought the gospel to their region of the world. Later, great Celtic saints like Aidan and Columba and Saint Patrick brought the gospel to the western part of the empire.

The gospel continued to spread across Persia and along the entire silk route that connected the Eastern Empire with the Far East. Remarkably, at the same time the gospel was being planted in England, it was also being presented by Nestorian missionaries right into the Imperial Court of China.

When Islam emerged in the seventh century, many former Christian lands fell and Christianity suffered a major setback in North Africa and what we now call the Middle East. Even the so-called Holy Land fell to Islam. But the light of the gospel could not be put out. Boniface brought the gospel into the heart of what is now Germany. Cyril and Methodius were translating the gospel into the Slavic tongue. Vladimir braved the mighty steppes of Russia to bring the gospel. Even in the darkest days of the Western attempt to militarily defeat Islam, known as the Crusades, there were faithful bearers of the gospel, like Raymond Lull, who brought the gospel to the seat of the Islamic empire in North Africa and was known as the apostle of love in an age of hate.

Eventually, the heart of the gospel message and the authority of the Scripture was recaptured by the European church in the Reformation. In due course, this gave birth to the modern missionary movement, first with the Moravians streaming forth from the estate of Count von Zinzendorf, and eventually with the rise of mission societies who sent men and women like William Carey, Adoniram Judson, Hudson Taylor, C. T. Studd, Amy Carmichael, Lottie Moon, and Gladys Alyward (and others too numerous to count to the ends of the earth). Africa buried the missionaries by the hundreds, earning the name of "the missionary graveyard" because the average lifespan of a missionary was only two years. But in the end, Christianity took root in the soil of Africa. China called the missionaries foreign devils, but the real story is that the gospel took root in Chinese soil, because the gospel is not western or eastern, it's the unfolding plan of God's redemption for the world. In this way the gospel spread all over the world!

This is God's unfolding story of redemption. From the remote islands of the Pacific to the breathtaking mountains of Nepal, this is God's story. From the Jesuit witness in the Imperial Court of China to the relentless travels of David Livingstone in the heart of Africa, this is God's story. From the work of Wycliffe Bible translators working in the tribal jungles of Papua New Guinea to many Asbury graduates working year after year in the great sprawling cities of the Muslim world like Istanbul, Cairo, Damascus, and Jakarta, this is God's story. From English classes being taught in the name of Jesus to the immigrant populations of North America to the fiery preaching on the streets of Rio or Sao Paulo in Latin America, this is God's story! From the church planters facing persecution in the heat of North India's Ganges plain to the bitter cold winds blowing across the faces of gospel workers in Mongolia, this is God's story. From the mass evangelistic campaigns of Billy Graham and Luis Pulau to a quiet moment as a young Russian girl kneels at her bedside and, with tears streaming down her cheeks, asks Jesus to save her, this is God's story.

Only eternity will tell the full story; we only know a few of the chapters of this great story of the church of Jesus Christ extending the good news of the risen Lord Jesus Christ as the Savior of the world. Are you part of this unfolding story?

We are all moving toward that great day when, in the apostle John's vision he captures a glimpse of the culmination of all human history: "After this I looked, and there before me was a great multitude that no one could count, from every nation, tribe, people and language, standing before the throne and before the Lamb" (Rev. 7:9a NIV).

— Chapter Three —

A Servant Body You Have Prepared for Me

Psalm 40; Hebrews 10:5–12

The Psalter is arranged in five books. One way of looking at the book of the Psalms is to see the entire collection as the sung Torah—the revelation of God in five books just like the Pentateuch. It is a very different experience to encounter the revelation of God not in legal codes or commandments, or even in historical narratives and bold prophecies from the lips of the great prophets of old, but in *sung worship*. We encounter God differently in worship than we do in texts, don't we? Singing is one of those grand gifts of God that brings together your mind, your heart, and your body in a dynamic unity which is almost without parallel. Thus, the book of Psalms invites us into a very different way of encountering God's Word. The Psalms or the sung Torah comes to us in 150 separate psalms that are like 150 preset life journeys covering the whole range of human experiences. While it is tempting to pluck favorite verses out of the Psalms like one of those promise boxes sold in Christian bookstores, the Psalms were not given to us to pluck out random verses and put them on our refrigerators or screen savers. There is, of course, no harm in that, but it is a bit outside the design. Each psalm invites us into a distinct journey of faith, each with its own special gifts for us.

Our focus in this chapter is on Psalm 40. When viewed through the widest vista of the 150 journeys, it is a bit unusual. Many psalms depict situations of trial, hardship, and even deep lament. Many psalms move us from peril to praise, or from hardship to hope, but Psalm 40 begins with the servant of God rejoicing in his deliverance. Verse 1: "I waited patiently for the LORD; he inclined to me and he heard my cry." Verse 2: "He drew me up from the pit of destruction, out of the miry bog, and set my feet upon a rock, making my steps secure." Verses 3–4a: "He put a new song in my mouth . . . Blessed is the man who makes the LORD his trust." Verses 4 and 5 go on to declare how the psalmist is trusting the Lord, and this part of the psalm climaxes with him extolling the wondrous deeds of the Lord. This psalm begins where some psalms end. It would not be difficult to turn the first five verses of this psalm into a worship song. But the journey of Psalm 40, like life, is a bit more complex.

Verses 6 and 7 of our psalm take an fascinating turn. I mentioned earlier how the Psalms often take biblical Law or Prophets and turn them into acts of worship. That happens here in Psalm 40 in a very interesting way. When you read a psalm, one of the ways to calibrate yourself into the journey is to think, conceptually, both backward and forward. You must think *back* on how this psalm enshrines something from the Pentateuch or Prophets, and only then think *forward* on how this psalm may be quoted and applied in the New Testament. So, let's do this together.

The leading way most psalms are structured from a strictly poetical point of view is through a poetical form called parallelism. In a typical traditional poem in the Western world, we think of sound rhyming as a key part of poetry. Open any hymnal at random and on almost any page you will see that the verses are actually poetry with each verse or half verse ending with a sound rhyme. This is the most basic form of poetry in the Western world.

Hebrew poetry doesn't work that way. Instead, Hebrew poetry is driven not by *sound* rhyming, but by *thought* rhyming, a form of parallelism. What is a thought rhyme? A thought rhyme is where you make a declaration, like the opening of Psalm 19 (NIV): "The heavens declare the glory of God" (v. 1a), and then you restate the same thought in a slightly different way: "the skies proclaim the work of his hands" (v. 1b). It states the basic thought in a fresh way, using different words. In Psalm 19, for example, different words are used to rhyme the thought with the words in the earlier line. Words and phrases like *heaven* and *expanse*, *declare* and *proclaim* and then "the glory of God" and "the work of his hands." These are examples of Hebrew parallelism in their poetry. There are dozens of variations of this which you will learn if you take time to really read the book of Psalms carefully.

Now, in its most basic form the thought rhyming happens one phrase right after another. But in Psalm 40 there is a variation where it gives a thought, and thought rhymes it at the end, but sticks another thought in between. Let's look at the basic thought rhyme of verse 6: "In sacrifice and offering you have not delighted . . ." This is thought rhymed with "Burnt offering and sin offering you have not required." These two phrases of verse 6 refer

A Servant Body You Have Prepared for Me

to an act of worship that reflects important theology from the Old Testament.

Your first reaction when you read this passage might be to say, "Wait a minute, what do you mean 'you have not *delighted* in sacrifice and offerings' and 'you have not *required* burnt offerings and sin offerings'? Lord, didn't you require burnt offerings and sin offerings? Why does this say you haven't required it, when you clearly did require it?" Leviticus 1, for example, sets forth the commands for burnt offerings. Leviticus 3 sets forth the commands for sin offerings.

But this psalm is not thought rhyming with Leviticus 1–3. Everyone who sang this psalm when it was composed and sung was a Jew who knew backward and forward that God desired and required sacrifices and sin offerings. But the thought rhyming here is with a whole different set of texts like 1 Samuel 15:22b: "to obey is better than sacrifice." And like the prophet Isaiah where God says, "I have had enough of burnt offerings . . . I do not delight in the blood of bulls, or of lambs, or of goats" (Isa. 1:11). Hosea 6:6 declares: "I desire mercy, not sacrifice" (NIV). There are many other passages like this in the Old Testament. In Psalm 40, all the theology of all those texts finds its way into this act of worship; Samuel and Isaiah and

Hosea all knew as well as the psalmist that these sacrifices and offerings had been commanded. But they were never an end in themselves. Religious activity in itself is worthless if it is not united with true devotion and an expression of the heart before God. So, looking backward, this psalm is seeking to capture those texts of Scripture that remind us that God doesn't need or require offerings in some mechanical sense. Indeed, all of the outward rituals and sacrifices of the Old Testament were always intended to point us onward to a greater fulfillment and a deeper transformation.

Now that we have looked backward, let's look forward. This odd middle phrase inserted between the two parallel phrases has many different translations: "you have given me an open ear" (Ps. 40:6b). Your translation may say, "my ears you have opened" (NIV) or perhaps a more literal translation of "you have pierced my ear" or "you have dug my ear." It is here that the psalm takes another interesting turn. Having put us on the page of thinking about the real intent of the sacrificial system, the psalmist reminds us that none of us has really ever made a proper sacrifice. "It is impossible for the blood of bulls and goats to take away sins" we are told in Hebrews 10:4 (NIV).

This Hebrew text in Psalm 40 literally says "my ears you have dug." Some early versions of NIV translated

A Servant Body You Have Prepared for Me

it "you have pierced my ears," which led people down a path thinking that this was about the Deuteronomy 15:17 passage where a servant would have his or her ears pierced if they pledged their life to the master. I don't think this text has anything to do with that. It is about creation. We were fashioned out of a lump of clay, and as a part of God fashioning our bodies, he dug out ears on the sides of our head so we could hear.

This is confirmed by the way this text is quoted in the New Testament. Hebrews 10:5–7 puts this psalm into the mouth of Jesus. The writer of Hebrews takes an old Jewish worship song and has Jesus singing it and applying the first-person language to himself. Hebrews 10 directly quotes Psalm 40:6–8 but powerfully introduces it by saying, "When Christ came into the world, he said . . ." (v. 5). And then Jesus speaks the words of Psalm 40:6–8.

You will notice that in the New Testament that middle phrase seems to be different: Psalm 40:6 had "you have given me an open ear." But in Hebrews 10:5 it says, "a body have you prepared for me." Why this big difference? The reason is that the early Jews of the New Testament did not read the Hebrew Old Testament, but rather used the Greek translation of the Old Testament called the Septuagint. The translators who put the Old Testament into Greek around the middle of the third century before Christ would sometimes bring out emphases to clarify the meaning just as we often do with modern translations. So, while the text literally says, "God dug the ears" as part of his creation, they wanted to make sure we realized that this was about God's full act in creation. Therefore, the deeper point in the passage is that he fashioned every part of us, not just our ears. He prepared our whole bodies. The Greek translators understood "ears" as a *synecdoche*, a fancy word which means that a part represents the whole. For example, if you remember saying to your parents years ago, "May I have the keys?" it was clear that what you really wanted was not the keys, but to use the car. In the same way, "God dug our ears" is by extension (or through synecdoche) "God dug and fashioned our whole bodies." Thus, "a body you have prepared for me."

The amazing application of this in Hebrews 10 is that the sacrifices were insufficient and, therefore, Christ came as the final sacrifice. That is a big part of the argument of Hebrews 10, which points to the heart of our redemption involving the "offering of the body of Jesus Christ once for all" (v. 10) and, "when Christ had offered for all time a single sacrifice for sins, he sat down at the right hand of God" (v. 12). The verse "Behold, I have come to do your

A Servant Body You Have Prepared for Me

will" (v. 7) is placed into a thought rhyme with "a body have you prepared for me" (v. 5). This text anticipates the incarnation whereby a body is prepared for Jesus Christ so he can come and do God's redemptive work in the world.

The writer piles up these amazing thought rhymes to draw us into the connection between Psalm 40 and the incarnation and sacrifice of Jesus Christ. The sacrifices of bulls and goats thought rhymes with the sacrifice of Jesus Christ. The declaration that God fashioned or dug out our ears thought thymes with our whole bodies being created by God and, ultimately, that God sent his only Son in bodily form through the incarnation to redeem us.

The wonder of creation that God could take a lump of clay and form our bodies so we can hear is thought rhymed with God's Son Jesus Christ becoming incarnate and hearing the will of God and obeying it! The Old Testament example of Jewish servants trying to serve God through sacrifices is thought rhymed with the one true Israelite, Jesus Christ, who is the true servant of God who offers the final sacrifice.

Verses 9 and 10 of Psalm 40 expand the scope from the servant to the whole congregation: "I have told the glad news of deliverance in the great congregation," and the parallel, "I have not concealed your steadfast love and your faithfulness from the great congregation." The idea is that at the dawn of creation God prepared our bodies in his creative act. But today, Jesus Christ is preparing an even greater body, the church of Jesus Christ. Those of us whose ears have been opened, not merely in the ordinary sense of hearing, but in the deeper sense of our spiritual awakening, to hear and obey (like Christ) the will of God in our lives is a very powerful application of this psalm for all of us.

Psalm 40 now takes another remarkable turn. All of this victory and celebration and proclamation is met with resistance. In verse 12, the psalm declares that "evils have encompassed me beyond number; my iniquities have overtaken me, and I cannot see; they are more than the hairs of my head; my heart fails me." The great messianic declaration of Psalm 40:6–8 now culminates in the raw challenge of a world trapped in sin and iniquity. This is another foretaste of the suffering and pain that the Servant endures for us. We know, of course, that Jesus Christ, the Servant of God, had come to bodily bear these iniquities which are more than the hairs of our head—a graphic metaphor for the pervasiveness of sin that does not merely impede us or slow us down, but has killed us. We are, in the words of Ephesians 2:1, "dead in [our] trespasses and sins," meaning that we lack the power to transform ourselves without the redemptive acts of God in prevenient grace, justifying grace, sanctifying grace, and someday, glorifying grace. The whole Wesleyan view of salvation is anticipated in this dilemma.

Finally, the journey of Psalm 40 ends with what has become the most powerful prayer of deliverance in the life of the church. We also encounter it as Psalm 70. This section of Psalm 40, which is in Book One of the psalms, gets repeated in Book Two as a stand-alone psalm. In other words, Psalm 40:13–17 *is* Psalm 70.

Saint John Cassian (360–435) was an early Christian writer from modern-day Romania who was fluent in both Greek and Latin, and so became revered in both the Eastern and Western church. Cassian took the opening line of Psalm 70 (or Psalm 40:13) and included it in the daily liturgy of the Egyptian-styled monastic order he established on the coast of France. Here is the prayer: "O God deliver me; O LORD, make haste to help me."

Cassian greatly influenced another monastic leader, Saint Benedict (480–543), who is revered as the father of the Benedictine monastic tradition and the famous "Rule of St. Benedict." Benedict required his monks to pray this prayer seven times per day. Centuries later, Archbishop Thomas Crammer took this same prayer from Psalm 40 and Psalm 70 and made it a daily prayer in the Anglican liturgy. Thus, this prayer became central to churches in the East and the West—Orthodox and Roman Catholic, and also in Protestant traditions across eighteen centuries. This makes it arguably the most prayed prayer in the whole life of the church across the world. It is our classic Servant Prayer as we daily ask God to help us to be his servants in the world.

What a journey this psalm brings us on, especially with the help of the writer of Hebrews who applies this psalm to the person and work of Jesus Christ. The psalm brings us on a journey from the Servant to the very nature of servanthood in the Christian vision. We are all poor and needy before the presence of God. We look to the incarnate one who embodied God's servanthood in the world and we say with the ages, "O God deliver me; O Lord, make haste to help me!"

── Chapter Four ──

The Two Songs of Servanthood

1 Samuel 2:1–10; Luke 1:26–38, 46–55

Several years ago, someone submitted a newly released Christian book to be reviewed. The reviewer wrote the following shocking and yet memorable words about the book: "A truly Christian book must contain three elements: color, fire, and music. Since this book contains neither color, nor fire, nor music, I must conclude that it is not even a Christian book." It is, of course, a devastating review. But it does point to a great insight about what happens when true Christianity touches anything, be it a person's life, a church, or even a book—it gives it color, fire, and music.

The two passages of Scripture we are meditating on here are filled with color, fire, and music in many profound ways. They are songs from two different testaments, sung at the two ends of the great prophetic stream. The first, from the lips of Hannah, is the first and earliest messianic song of expectation. The second, from the lips of Mary, is the final and culminating messianic song at the point of fulfillment. Both songs pour forth from two women at two ends of prophetic history. Both are marvelous embodiments of servanthood on the two ends of this great stream we call "salvation history."

We should envision this great stream of the prophets from Samuel to John the Baptist like a long rope that stretches from the dawn of prophetic expectation to the high noon of prophetic fulfillment. Along that rope lie all the great prophetic hopes, dreams, longings, and expectations. The rope stretches out over a thousand years. The prophet Isaiah is on that rope as he foretells the coming of Immanuel and the one called "Wonderful Counselor, Mighty God, Everlasting Father, Prince of Peace" (Isa. 9:6). The prophet Jeremiah is on that great rope as he foretells the coming of the "righteous Branch" who will bring us a "new covenant" (Jer. 23:5; 31:31). The prophet Ezekiel is on that rope as he foretells the coming of the servant shepherd (Ezek. 34). Daniel is on that rope as well. He looks for a "Son of Man" who will be "given dominion and glory and a kingdom," and "all peoples, nations, and languages" will worship him (Dan. 7:13–14). And on and on it goes, all through Old Testament history, each prophet anticipated the coming of the Messiah. Each one had his own insights into the true majesty of the Messiah. But the entire rope is being held on either end by two women, Hannah and Mary. They are the ones God chose to hold the two ends of the rope.

Song of Hannah

We will begin this chapter by looking back at the first song, the Song of Hannah. Hannah was a Jewish woman who lived at a time of great spiritual darkness. First Samuel 3:1 says that "the word of the LORD was rare." It was a tough time. Hope was in short supply. Yet, out of the darkness came color, fire, and music, pouring forth from the heart of Hannah. It is the first messianic song in the Bible.

It is from Hannah's barren womb that the first Old Testament prophet was born: Samuel. The name Samuel means "God heard." What did God hear? God heard the prayer of Hannah, which is recorded poetically as a song in the Bible. It was in response to her messianic cry that God set into motion the people and events that would finally culminate in the incarnation of Jesus Christ through the womb of Mary. We still sing about this great story. Charles Wesley gave us those words:

> Veiled in flesh the Godhead see,
> hail th'incarnate Deity!
> Pleased as man with men to dwell,
> Jesus, our Immanuel![3]

Yes, the songs still go on, but Hannah's was the first. The song of Hannah is about hope. Hope is believing in something that hasn't happened yet. Hope is about what can happen with small beginnings and sincere prayers. Hannah is in despair over her barren womb. Bearing children has always been a sign of fruitfulness and the blessing of God. Hannah was barren. Her own barrenness seemed to reflect the spiritual barrenness that was all around her. Eli, the priest of Shiloh, was so spiritually barren that he interpreted Hannah's agonizing prayers not as earnest prayers, but as intoxicated mutterings (1 Sam. 1:13). Eli's sons, who represented the future of the priesthood, are

---

3. Charles Wesley, "Hark! The Herald Angels Sing," public domain.

described as wicked. The Bible openly acknowledges that they "did not know the LORD" (1 Sam. 2:12). In short, there are no prophets. There is no word from the Lord. The priesthood had become corrupt. The whole history of redemption hung upon the prayers of Hannah. Hannah was holding the end of the rope. All of us should thank God that Hannah didn't let go of that rope. She prayed. She trusted. She sang. In this process she became one of the great models for us to understand servanthood.

A servant of God is someone who lives in the hope of God, even in the midst of a world that has lost hope. Servanthood in the biblical vision is always linked to hope, which is why we can descend into the darkest places and not lose faith in the goodness of God or the power of the gospel. Hannah's song anticipates great things happening in the world not through human strength, not through human ingenuity, not through human power, but through God's Anointed One. She looks to the day when the Messiah would come. This is the first time the word *messiah* is explicitly used in the Bible. It is the Hebrew word for "anoint." This is the same word that is translated in Greek as "Christ." Hannah is inspired to see that the hope of the world was not in priestly anointing but in a person, an Anointed One. She begins the whole focus of the prophetic stream by looking not to ritual acts, but looking for a person.

Hannah envisions the day as already present when the Messiah would bring about a great reversal. In 1 Samuel 2:4 she says that "the bows of the warriors are broken, but those who stumbled are armed with strength" (NIV). In verse 5 she envisions a day when "those who were full hire themselves out for food, but those who were hungry are hungry no more" (NIV). It is a picture of God coming to judge the world, and setting things right. Even in her own barrenness she has the faith to declare: "She who was barren has borne seven children, but she who has had many sons pines away" (v. 5b). She longs for the day when the Messiah will come and interrupt the endless flow of evil and wickedness in the world and assert his rightful claim on the peoples of the earth.

For Hannah, the universe is not the result of some chance collision of molecules. The social status of the world is not shaped by mindless economic forces. History is not the result of mere dialectical materialism or sociocultural evolution. Behind all human history stands the God of the universe who is sovereign. It is to God that Hannah directs her amazing prayer. She held onto that rope when no one else had the courage to think like this, or pray like this, or sing like this. Hannah's song is filled with declarations that place God as the subject: "The LORD brings death and makes alive" (v. 6 NIV). "The LORD sends" (v. 7 NIV). The Lord "raises up" (v. 8). The Lord guards his people (v. 9). He thunders from heaven. He judges. He gives strength. Finally, it is he who sends his Anointed One.

For Hannah, God takes orders from no one. He was created by no one. He remembers nothing because he has forgotten nothing. He learns nothing because there is nothing he does not know. He does not need to recall because he holds all truth simultaneously. He is the God of the eternal now. Every point in history is eternally present to him. He can look at human history from the beginning or the end or the middle, for all things are known to him. And he stood by a Jewish woman one day and inspired her to utter something in hope and in expectation that at the time seemed impossible. She dared to believe that "with God all things are possible" (Matt. 19:26).

No one realized that Hannah was holding the end of a prophetic rope that would someday lead to the incarnation, the church of Jesus Christ, and be fully realized in that great day when men and women from every tribe, language, tongue will shout, "Hallelujah! For the Lord our God the Almighty reigns" and "the kingdom of the world has become the kingdom of our Lord and of his Christ, and he shall reign forever and ever" (Rev. 19:6; 11:15). The priest who saw this prayer thought she was drunk; he couldn't hear the song. But God heard the song.

Out of the haltering lips of a Jewish woman came pouring forth the good news of God's Messiah, God's Anointed One. Hannah dared to believe that if God can turn the barrenness of her womb into the fruitfulness of a little boy named Samuel, then he can turn the barrenness of our ugly sinful world into the fruitfulness of God's visitation. Hannah articulated at the very beginning of the prophetic stream what would happen when the Messiah stepped into the world. Everything would be turned upside down. Against all odds, she held onto her end of the rope and sang her song, which was embodied in the birth of Samuel, who would be the progenitor of that great prophetic messianic stream.

Song of Mary: The Magnificat

The same God who heard Hannah's prayer stood at the other end of that stream with a young Jewish woman named Mary; two Jewish women whom the world would have regarded as powerless at each end of the rope.

The Two Songs of Servanthood

Mary's song, the Magnificat, is one of the most ancient Christian hymns since it is recorded in the New Testament and appears in the very first chapter of Luke's Gospel (1:46–55). The Magnificat is preceded by Gabriel's annunciation to Mary. The annunciation to Mary probably deserves its own separate chapter, but we are going to focus on Mary's Magnificat. Just try to put yourself in young Mary's sandals, and the angel Gabriel has just appeared to you, and told you the following seven things:

"Mary, you have found favor with God." (v. 30)
"You will conceive in your womb and bear a son." (v. 31)
"He will be called the Son of the Most High." (v. 32)
"The Lord God will give to him the throne of his father David . . ." (v. 32)
". . . and of his kingdom there will be no end." (v. 33)
"The Holy Spirit will come upon you, and the power of the Most High will overshadow you." (v. 35)
"The child to be born will be called holy—the Son of God." (v. 35)

Just think about that! Mary's response is why I chose this text for helping us to understand servanthood better. Mary said, "Behold, I am the servant of the Lord; let it be to me according to your word" (v. 38). Behold Mary, the servant of the Lord. She stands at the other end of the rope looking back across the centuries to that other great servant of the Lord, Hannah, who was holding the other end of the rope.

Mary's Song begins, as Hannah's did, with an act of worship: "My soul magnifies the Lord, and my spirit rejoices in God my Savior" (Luke 1:46–47). Mary declares that "all generations will call me blessed" (v. 48). Mary is blessed not only because she has been chosen to bear the Messiah, but also because she has been chosen to hold the other end of this great prophetic rope. She will be blessed because she will be on the right side of this "great reversal" which Hannah first spoke of more than one thousand years earlier. Mary goes on to articulate the "great reversal" with language very similar to Hannah's: "He has performed mighty deeds with his arm; he has scattered those who are proud" (v. 51 NIV). "He has brought down rulers from their thrones but has lifted up the humble" (v. 52 NIV). "He has filled the hungry with good things but has sent the rich away empty" (v. 53 NIV).

Mary's humble estate was mirrored by Jesus Christ himself who came not to Plato's Academy, nor to Herod's Palace. He did not even come into the world in the Jewish temple. Rather, he came to us in a lowly stable, born as a Jew, born under oppression, soon to be a refugee. Who would have believed that this birth was the hope of the world? Yet, somehow, Hannah and Mary knew. Mary is announcing the arrival of this Great Reversal.

Mary knows that history will not turn on decisions made by U.S. or Chinese presidents, or by British or Indian prime ministers. History, for Mary, as with Hannah, is directed by God on the throne! James Lowell captured this truth so well in his hymn, "Once to Every Man and Nation." The hymn concludes this way:

> Though the cause of evil prosper,
> Yet 'tis truth alone is strong;
> Though her portion be the scaffold,
> And upon the throne be wrong:
> Yet that scaffold sways the future,
> And, behind the dim unknown,
> Standeth God within the shadow
> Keeping watch above His own.[4]

Yes, the song continues to be sung, as we, too, anticipate the final climax of the ages when Christ will return and set all things right. We are now in a season of grace to

---

4. James Lowell, "Once to Every Man and Nation," 1845, public domain.

gather as many as will come into God's rule and reign. But, in God's own time, the curtain of history will someday fall, and we will all be called to give an account of our lives and hopes. We want to be marked by servanthood, seeing with hope that which is yet to come. "Lord, 'let it be to me according to your word'" (Luke 1:38). That's the prayer of a servant. It is mirrored in that great Wesleyan Covenant Prayer:

> I am not my own. I am Yours alone.
> Make me into what You will.
> Rank me with those You will.
> Put me to use for You.
> Put me to suffering for You.
> Let me be employed by You.
> Let me be laid aside for You.
> Let me be lifted high for You.
> Let me be brought low for You.
> Let me be full or let me be empty.
> Let me have all things or let me have nothing.[5]

If you can pray a prayer like that, you are putting your hand on that rope. You are now connected to the Vine.

---

5. *Asbury Hymnal* (Franklin, TN: Seedbed Publishing, 2018), xxi.

The Two Songs of Servanthood

Your life will be filled with color, fire, and music as we join in with these two dear women of faith, Hannah and Mary. We, too, must put our hand on the rope and lay claim to this great message which is for the world. We must join in that great song that Jesus himself is singing. It is a song filled with color, fire, and music.

Chapter Five

Servanthood in the "Other" Parable of the Two Sons

MATTHEW 21:28–32, 33–46; 22:1–14;
LUKE 15:11–32

This chapter seeks to explore what makes Christian servanthood distinctive in the world. In this chapter we will look at three of the eight parables in Matthew's Gospel which are found only in his Gospel: the parable of the two sons, the parable of the tenants, and the parable of the wedding feast. We will begin with the parable of the two sons. When we think of the parable of the two sons, our minds generally go to the parable of the lost son or prodigal son, which is only found in Luke's Gospel. But this is a different parable, even though it also involves two sons. That is why this chapter is called the "other" parable of the two sons, although we are going to show how these two parables relate to one another.

Parable of the Two Sons

In this parable Jesus speaks of a man who has two sons. "He went to the first and said, 'Son, go and work in the vineyard today'" (Matt. 21:28), and the son answered, "'I will not,' but afterward he changed his mind and went" (v. 29). He gave the same directive to his other son who answered, "'I go, sir,' but did not go" (v. 30). Jesus asks the question: "Which of the two did the will of his father?" (v. 31).

Most of you who are reading this chapter will know that the underlying power of all the parables is that they play on some tension, which when brought to the surface, reveals the deeper kingdom ethic that Jesus is seeking to highlight. On the surface, this parable seems to be lacking that tension, so it requires some explanation for us to get the point. When we hear Jesus's question, "Which of the two did the will of his father?" (v. 31), it seems to be the closest thing we can find in the New Testament to a no-brainer. However, this is not the case in a shame-based culture in which the New Testament was rooted, both Jewish and Greek. In that context it is a viable question

Servanthood in the "Other" Parable of the Two Sons

because the second son, though he did not actually go and work in the vineyard, honored his father to his face by saying he would; whereas the first son, though he actually obeyed, shamed his father's face at the outset of the directive by saying bluntly to his face that he would not do it. So, to the original hearers, the tension is real because it is a tension between publicly honoring his father versus publicly shaming him and between obedience versus disobedience to the father. Mediterranean culture made two demands of a son: that they obey their father and that they honor them, and not shame them. These two values are put in tension in this parable.

It is clear, as in many of the parables of Jesus, the sons are representative of larger dynamics playing out in the ministry of Jesus. In that sense, there really is a parallel between both parables of the sons. Like these three parables in Matthew, which come in quick succession, Luke also gives us three parables consecutively, all making the same point using different images: the parable of the lost sheep, the parable of the lost coin, and the parable of the prodigal son (Luke 15). In the Lukan parable of the prodigal son, the father represents God; the older son, the Jewish leadership; and the younger son, the wayward sinners. In the parable, the older son gave lip service to the father (God), but never really knew the heart of the father (God); and the younger son (who outwardly rebelled but later repented) represents the sinners who discover the true heart of the father (God). The younger son, you will recall, shamed his father by asking for his share of the inheritance. It was like saying to your own father, "I wish you were dead." Notice that he both disobeys his father and shames him as he takes his inheritance and goes off to a faraway country.

Parable of the Lost Sons (or Prodigal Son)

You will recall that when the prodigal repented in the faraway country he devised one of the first three-point sermons in the history of homiletics. Point one: "Father I have sinned against heaven and before you" (Luke 15:18). Point two: "I am no longer worthy to be called your son" (v. 19a). Point three: "Treat me as one of your hired servants" (v. 19b). In some ways, this is the standard three-point sermon of the religions of the world. I am a sinner; I am not worthy to be called your son; make me a hired hand for God.

But the gospel operates on a different plane. The first two points are true. We are sinners and we are not worthy to be called the sons and daughters of God. But in the end,

Servanthood in the "Other" Parable of the Two Sons

the answer is not being a hired hand for God, but being overcome by love of the Father and experiencing a restored relationship with him.

In the Luke 15 passage, the father runs to meet his son. In the ancient world a man of dignity did not run. Ben Sirah said, "By the way a man walks you know his true dignity." If you have a long gown on it is difficult to run, so you have to pick up your garment and humiliate yourself by running. It is a picture of the shame taken on by God in expressing the depth of his love for lost humanity.

The passage uses the word that in other parts of the New Testament describes Jesus's own heart for the world; the father is filled with *compassion*. The word used there is the Greek word *splagnizomoi,* which is related to our word for "spleen." In the ancient world it was recognized that the spleen is the deepest organ in the body. So this is why this word is sometimes translated "he was deeply moved" or, more commonly, "filled with compassion."

When the son returned from the distant country and his father ran to meet him, the son only got out the first two points: "Father, I have sinned against heaven and before you. I am no longer worthy to be called your son" (v. 21). But before he could get out the third point, "Treat me as one of your hired servants" (v. 19b), the gospel interrupts him and he is, in the surprise turn of the parable, reinstated as a full son, with robe, ring, sandals, and the glorious banquet reception with a fattened calf.

The gospel knows that you will never hate your sin enough to leave it, but if you can be loved enough, and really hear that, then you can go and sin no more. The younger son discovers the gospel in the arms of his father. The older son, though having never left his father's estate, saw himself as a hired hand: "All of these years I have slaved for you," he said, "whereas this 'son of yours' [he distances himself from the sonship of his younger brother] has prostituted himself, and yet you treat him as a son" (vv. 29–30, paraphrased).

This is why the parable should not be called the parable of the prodigal son, but rather the parable of the lost sons (plural) because, in the end, it was the older son who was lost, not the younger. It could also be appropriately called the parable of the waiting father because one of the great truths of the story is God's inestimable patience as he waits upon us to return to his arms and be embraced by the liberating power of the gospel. The younger son may have had a delayed obedience, but in the end, he was the son who was reconciled to his father. These two sons reflect the two groups hearing this parable in Luke's Gospel, "the

Pharisees and the scribes" (v. 2) and the "tax collectors and sinners" (v. 1). The former group was giving lip service to obedience but was, in fact, rejecting God's Messiah. The latter group, though sinners, marginalized and considered to be far from God, were actually joyfully responding to God's Messiah.

The Three Parables in Matthew

In many ways Matthew's parable of the two sons has many parallels. The son who gave lip service was not actually obeying, and the son who was belligerent, but later repented, ended up in the joyful company of the obedient. The lip-service son is like the religious authorities. They seem to conform to all the outward, public affirmations of ones dedicated to the service of God. "Yes, sir, I will go," the son said, but he didn't actually go. The other son, who dishonored the father to his face, later repented, and actually ended up serving the father. The delayed obedience is honored because, in the end, that's what matters. Obedience, not empty promise, is the key.

Notice in the passage that the son who originally said, "I will not," is said to have "changed his mind" (Matt. 21:29). The word used here means a transformational repentance that leads to thinking differently about things. It corresponds to that moment in the parable of the two lost sons where the prodigal son, longing to fill his stomach with the pods the pigs were eating, "came to his senses" (Luke 15:17 NIV). It is a moment of spiritual awakening where you realize the true state of affairs between yourself and God. But, as in the Lukan parable, the two sons represent two groups: the religious authorities who were big on lip service, while rejecting the Messiah, and feeling incensed by the responsiveness of the "tax collectors and sinners" and the religious outcasts who were joyfully hearing the gospel as good news (Luke 15:1–2). The parable pictures God the Father approaching the despicable spiritual outsiders with the invitation and they said no but "came to their senses" and returned to the Father. He gave the same invitation to the spiritual insiders, who gave lip service and said yes, but walked away.

One can't help but remember that amazing passage in the Prophets where God spoke through the prophet Isaiah and said about the people of God: "[They] honor me with their lips, while their hearts are far from me" (Isa. 29:13). This is the text that Jesus is powerfully expounding in parable form. Or, perhaps, he is expounding Ezekiel 33:31, where the Lord says to Ezekiel,

Servanthood in the "Other" Parable of the Two Sons

"they sit before you as my people, and they hear what you say but they will not do it."

Notice the exact wording Jesus uses as he opens up the meaning of this parable: "Truly, I say to you, the tax collectors and the prostitutes go into the kingdom of God before you" (Matt. 21:31). He doesn't use the more gentle phrase "kingdom of heaven," which is common in Matthew's Gospel, but rather "kingdom of God" to really drive home the point that they are not just rejecting some new religious movement, but they are rejecting God himself, who is represented by the father in both of these parables. This parable is a wake-up call to those of us who may feel that we have an inside track on God's work or who may find ourselves resistant to God's grace, while looking down on those who up to this point have rejected him.

I mentioned at the beginning of this chapter that we are going to look at three parables only found in Matthew's Gospel. These three parables belong together because they all carry a similar theme. We have examined the parable of the two sons (Matt. 21:28–32). The next parable (vv. 33–46) is about a farmer (who represents God) who loves his vineyard. The text is full of verbs reflecting God's prior action in caring for his vineyard (his people): he planted, he built a wall, he dug and fertilized, he entrusted it to tenants who were to care for its fruit, he sent servants to bring in the fruit. It is a picture of radical, biblical love like that of the Father running to his prodigal son with compassion and love.

The people of God just kept killing his servants one after another, but he kept sending them, and they kept killing them. The servants are, of course, the prophets. If the parable of the prodigal son could be called the parable of the waiting father, this one could be called the parable of the persistent father. He kept persisting in his covenant love, but they wouldn't have it. Finally, he sends his own Son. Surely, he thinks, they will respect him. The Son, you will recall from the first chapter in this book, is the fulfillment of the Servant of God theme in the Old Testament. God sends his ultimate Servant, his beloved Son. But they kill him too.

Their irrational rejection of God's love is met head-on by the equally irrational and radical extension of God's love. God's own Son steps right into the sinful, broken, bloody cycle of violence and hatred that characterizes this world. He throws out the established people of God and ordains a new people of God. The outcasts become those favored because, though late to the call, they saw in the Son the good news of God's love.

Servanthood in the "Other" Parable of the Two Sons

The same thing happens in the third parable, the story of the wedding banquet (22:1–14). God is pictured here as a king hosting a wedding. We are now being brought into a cosmic love story. God is calling his people to the wedding banquet. Yet they keep refusing to come. Like the vineyard, he tells his servants to put everything aside and come to the banquet. Remember how even in the parable of the prodigal son, the older son was also invited to join the banquet. However, this parable shrewdly shows how the rejection actually happens. They make excuses: "I would love to come, but I have to work in my farm," and "I would love to come, but I have some business to attend to" (v. 5, paraphrased). But finally, their real intent is clear. They seize the king's servants, beat them, and kill them.

So the king comes and destroys them and then sends out new invitations: "Go out to the roads, the highways and byways, and invite everyone in who will come, for my banquet hall will be filled" (v. 9, paraphrased). The hall is filled with guests, but, in a final twist, someone comes to the banquet who is not dressed in a wedding garment: "Friend, how did you get in here without a wedding garment?" (v. 12). The man was speechless. However, rather than him being joyfully embraced as you might expect after all of these parables about the lost sheep, the lost coin, and the lost sons, this wedding guest intruder is bound hand and foot and cast out into utter darkness where there will be "weeping and gnashing of teeth" (v. 13). Let's take some time to explore why this parable has this surprising ending.

The parable of the wedding banquet has a great lesson for us as we pursue this theme of servanthood. Servanthood in the New Testament is not about outward show but about actual obedience. Today, it is customary to talk a lot about servanthood and about service in the community and in the world, but it doesn't always translate into actual obedient action in the world. We want to be those who understand that servanthood, in the end, is about obedience to the Master. This is where we need to hear the message of the one who showed up to the banquet without wedding clothes.

The message in the parable of the sons as well as the two subsequent parables about the tenants in the vineyard and the wedding banquet, is that this grace is not cheap. We have to have a radical, universal, loving, and gracious call of God. But, even if we recognize the grace of God, we cannot show up on our own terms. He doesn't tell the man, "No worries, at least you came, come on into the banquet." No, the man must be properly clothed, which brings in the whole ethic of clothing that fills the New Testament (e.g., Col. 3:12).

This is where our Wesleyan message shines bright in the face of some versions of "cheap grace" or "grace alone." The powerful and beautiful call to God, "Just as I am, without one plea,"[6] which is intended to emphasize the free, unearned gift of salvation, can sometimes get twisted up to sound like, "Just come the way you are, and stay the way you are" because we have a kingdom of grace. No, grace comes and meets us with the radical call to transformation, which is the real sign of servanthood.

We must take off our soiled clothes of racism. We must leave behind our garments of bitterness and unforgiveness and pride. We must leave behind our self-righteousness, our anger, our rage. The garments of secret sin that we like to wear beneath our wedding clothes must be taken off. The radical call of discipleship requires us to cast off the garments of lust, of materialism, of marital unfaithfulness, of dishonesty, of contempt for those who don't share our political persuasions, and on and on it goes. We must not allow any identities to eclipse our deepest identity of being "in Christ."

---

6. Charlotte Elliott, "Just As I Am, Without One Plea," 1835, public domain.

We must take seriously the severe warning of Christ to us all; namely, that we count the cost of what it means to follow Christ as his servants in the world (Luke 14:25–35). Mere words will not suffice. We must become his servants in our daily lives, our deeds, our thoughts. Servanthood is precisely that place where the free gift of grace meets the cost of discipleship. This doesn't make us into spiritual superstars, but it does make us into a new creation through the power of the Holy Spirit. It is, after all, the heart of servanthood to align ourselves fully with God's Servant, Jesus Christ.

Many of you have had a long and twisting road, sometimes with periods where you moved in the opposite direction, but in the end, here you are, serving the Master. Today, I hope that you are rejoicing in the amazing grace of God who has "called you out of darkness into his marvelous light" (1 Peter 2:9)! I hope that every one of us never loses sight of the amazing grace of God which has made us daughters and sons of the almighty God, and given us the opportunity to serve him in his kingdom.

— Chapter Six —

Servanthood in the Storm

PSALM 89

Our daughter, Bethany, has spent more than twelve years bringing the gospel to the Alagwa people in North Central Tanzania. They are 99.9 percent Muslim, extremely resistant, and don't speak the language of the larger country, which is Swahili. Therefore, they are effectively cut off from the church in their own country. Their language, Alagwisa, is not even in the same language group as Swahili. The story of the last twelve years of Bethany's life is mostly a story of people rejecting the gospel in a seemingly never-ending array of ways.

The Life of Servanthood

In her first ten years there, many well-meaning people would assure her by saying, "Remember, it's not your job to bring the Alagwa to Christ; you just do your part and God will do his part." Bethany wondered for years why God didn't seem to be doing his part. Surely, he loved them more than she did. Why were there no signs of any response? Instead, without any even glimmers of hope, she hit a brick wall day after day, week after week, month after month, year after year.

It was in about her tenth year that the Lord helped Bethany to see that all these years he was actually answering her prayers. Her deepest prayer was that she wanted to be a co-laborer with Christ. Her greatest prayer was to be in union with Jesus. She has renounced all the comforts of this world, has no running water, no electricity, no stores to buy food, etc. She has long ago given up on marriage. She just wants to be united to Christ in his mission to the Alagwa. That's her passion.

Gradually, after more than a decade, it dawned on her that this idea of "you do your part and God does his part" was one of the greatest misunderstandings and false dichotomies of the modern church. Because her part *is* united to God's part. God's part *is* united to her part. They are united in this mission. What Bethany realized was that to be truly united to Christ, she had to be united to him in his sufferings. The rejection she gets every day amongst the Alagwa is nothing less than the very rejection God experiences every day all over the world. To be with God in the world is to be rejected; so, if we want to be united to him, we must be prepared to bear the cross of pain, rejection, public shaming, gossip, and all that goes with that union. This is why God gives us psalms like Psalm 89.

John Goldingay, Old Testament scholar and the author of a massive three-volume commentary on the Psalms, was once asked why there are 150 psalms in the collection. He said, "Apparently, to provide God's people with 150 examples of things one can say to God." That's a nice, succinct way of putting it, but I think it might be helpful to say it a little differently: the Psalms are, at root, a collection of 150 life journeys, each with a divinely appointed lesson for those who would tread this path of faith, and unite themselves to this surprising God of biblical revelation. If you see these as invitations into a life journey, then each psalm is like a divinely appointed Sherpa to expertly guide us down a particular path where we learn what it really means to be the servant of God.

If the Psalms are like preset life journeys, then Psalm 89 is a one-of-a-kind doozy! Psalm 89 invites us into a very disruptive and painful journey. It is one of those psalms that we might easily just skip over and fast-forward to Psalm 100 or another favorite. It is one of the great ironies of the modern chorus movement that the first verse of this psalm was at one time at the top of the ten greatest hits in the church worship charts with the well-known, joyful chorus: "I will sing of the mercies of the Lord forever" (Ps. 89:1a, paraphrased). But the actual journey of this psalm, if you have the courage to take it all the way to verse 51, is one of the most disturbing and disruptive psalms in the Psalter. You may notice that I said to verse 51, not verse 52. This psalm does contain 52 verses, but in this case, it is actually important to understand that verse 52 is not part of this psalm per se, but is a closing doxology that is added to bring the entire book to a close, according to Jewish practice. This is the last psalm of Book 3 of the Psalter. This is a feature of the end of Psalm 41, 72, 89, and 106, which are the seams between the books, and Psalm 150 in its entirety is probably an expanded doxology for all five books of the Psalter or "Sung Torah." It reminds us that the five collections of psalms in five separate books once had a life and circulation apart from the others.

The reason this is important for Psalm 89 is that it becomes one of only four psalms in the Bible that leaves us with no resolution. Psalm 89 ends with the soul-wrenching taunts and insults of the enemy. Psalm 88 ends with those chilling words: "darkness is my closest friend" (v. 18 NIV). If you have ever been to a Tenebrae service during Lent, you will know that after each reading, more lights are diminished until, in the end, you are sitting in complete darkness and you are often instructed to leave the sanctuary in complete silence. It is a service that seeks to help us experience that sense of abandonment, the agony of God's silence, the reality that many of us experience when we have so many questions for God about why certain things have happened in our lives, but we are left without clear answers. It is tempting to grasp at some glib, trite, easy answer when we are called to sit in the darkness and be united with Christ in his own anguish and sense of separation from God.

Psalm 89 is the only psalm in the whole collection attributed to Ethan the Ezrahite. We know very little about Ethan the Ezrahite, but by combing through the various references to him (there are eight references to him in the Bible), we do learn a few things. First, he was a gifted worship leader, because he is mentioned as someone who was appointed to lead the worship of Israel. Second, we learn that Ethan played the bronze cymbals in the ancient

Levitical worship band (1 Chron. 15:19). In that text David told the Levites to appoint singers to sing the worship songs and to accompany with musical instruments: lyres, harps, and cymbals. Verse 17 starts listing names of those they appointed. In verse 19 it says, "The musicians Heman, Asaph and Ethan were to sound the bronze cymbals" (NIV). Third, we can determine from the genealogies that the two musicians Heman and Ethan are brothers, and Asaph is a cousin. Music runs in families. Fourth, he must have been known for his wisdom. I say this because, in 1 Kings 4, they are extolling the wisdom of Solomon. If someone says, "Hey, they can hit the ball better than Derek Jeter," it says a lot about them, but also a lot about Derek Jeter. The text says, "Solomon's wisdom surpassed . . . all the people of the east . . . For he was wiser than all other men, wiser than Ethan the Ezrahite" (vv. 30–31)! Ethan must be in the Solomonic range or they wouldn't have compared him in the first place.

The first part of the journey in Psalm 89 begins by reminding us who God is. He is not like the gods of the nations who are fickle, unreliable, and untrustworthy. This is the covenant-making creator God of the universe! Ethan calls forth two of the great building blocks of God's character revealed in Scripture. The first is the Hebrew word *hesed*, which is translated in various ways including goodness, kindness, and covenant love. The second is the Hebrew word *emunah,* which is translated as firmness, steadfastness, fidelity. Psalm 89, despite its painful direction, begins by Ethan the Ezrahite declaring, "I will sing of the steadfast love of the LORD, forever; with my mouth I will make known your faithfulness to all generations" (v. 1). He repeats the words for even greater emphasis in verse 2.

Now that he has laid the foundation of God's character (who he *is*), he focuses in verse 3 on what God has *done*—the covenant—"You have said, 'I have made a covenant with my chosen one; I have sworn to David my servant.'" Then, he gives the famous promise: "I will establish your offspring forever, and build your throne for all generations" (v. 4), a reference back to God's covenant to David in 2 Samuel 7:8–16.

The second part of the journey brings together the first two points; namely, God's character with how he has acted in history with covenant faithfulness. The psalm launches into a sweeping survey of God's sovereignty over the whole created order and his faithfulness in the history of Israel (vv. 5–18). Who can compare to Yahweh? Who is like the Lord? (v. 6). He rules the raging sea, he stills the angry waves, verse 9 declares. The sea in Jewish poetry represents chaos and fear; God is greater even than the uncertainty and power of the seas. "You crushed Rahab like a carcass; you scattered your enemies with your mighty arm" (v. 10). Rahab was a mythical sea creature like Leviathan, but in poetry it often refers to Egypt. This part of the psalm celebrates God's character by bringing out even more of the great covenant words: "Righteousness and justice are the foundation of your throne; steadfast love and faithfulness go before you" (v. 14). These are the solid, steadfast things that form the foundation of a faithful Jewish person walking in covenant with Yahweh.

Ethan then turns to God's promises to David: David was anointed by God, his kingdom was established, and he crushed all of his enemies. The psalm rehearses twelve great truths of God's covenant with David:

1. I have exalted and chosen him (v. 19).
2. "With my holy oil I have anointed him" (v. 20).
3. My hand and my arm will be with him (v. 21).
4. I will crush his foes and strike down those who oppose him (v. 23).
5. My faithfulness and steadfast love will be with him (v. 24).

6. "I will set his hand on the sea and his right hand on the rivers. He shall cry to me, 'You are my father, my God, and the Rock of my salvation'" (vv. 25–26).
7. "I will make him the firstborn, the highest of the kings of the earth" (v. 27).
8. "My steadfast love I will keep for him forever, and my covenant will stand firm for him" (v. 28).
9. "I will establish his offspring forever and his throne as the days of the heavens" (v. 29).
10. Even if his children sin, I will punish them, but I will not remove my steadfast love from David (vv. 30–33).
11. "I will not violate my covenant or alter the word that went forth from my lips" (v. 34).
12. His offspring will endure forever, his throne long as the sun or moon. It shall be established forever (vv. 36–37).

This is an unprecedented sweep of covenantal history related to David, all carefully tied into the known character qualities of God. All five of the key words that are often used to describe God's character and covenant are remembered: *love*, *truth*, *justice*, *righteousness*, and *faithfulness*.

This is the point where we enter into the third and final phase of this journey. The word *selah* is there to mark the important shift here. We are not certain what the word *selah* means. It occurs seventy-one times in the Psalms, appearing in thirty-nine of the psalms. It may be some kind of musical notation for an interlude, or it may indicate a pause before a tone shift. Perhaps it is both. But there is no doubt that the tone of the psalm dramatically shifts at this point.

The twelve affirmations of the vision are now poetically balanced by twelve disruptive accusations:

1. "You have cast off and rejected" us (v. 38).
2. "You are full of wrath against your anointed" (v. 38).
3. "You have renounced the covenant" (v. 39).
4. "You have defiled his crown in the dust" (v. 39).
5. "You have breached all his walls [and] laid his strongholds in ruins" (v. 40).
6. You have allowed him to be plundered and scorned by his neighbors (v. 41).
7. "You have exalted the right hand of his foes" (v. 42).
8. "You have made all his enemies rejoice" (v. 42).
9. "You have also turned back the edge of the sword, and you have not made him stand in battle" (v. 43).
10. "You have made his splendor to cease and cast his throne to the ground" (v. 44).

11. "You have cut short the days of his youth" (v. 45).

12. "You have covered him with shame" (v. 45).

Then the word *selah* appears again. The psalmist wants us to pause and to sit for a minute in the tension between God's amazing and trustworthy promises and yet, at the same time, the feeling we all have when we don't seem to see those promises in our lives, in the church, or in the world.

To put it bluntly, the psalmist feels like God has not kept his side of the covenant. He senses God's anger. He sees his strongholds reduced to ruins. Everywhere he looks he sees the people of God defeated and plundered. The psalmist is distraught. He feels like God has forgotten him and his people. It seems to him that God has renounced the covenant. Have you ever felt that way? The psalm then breaks into a series of questions which are almost shouted out at God:

1. "How long, O Lord?" (v. 46).
2. "Will you hide yourself forever?" (v. 46).
3. "How long will your wrath burn like fire?" (v. 46).
4. "What man can live and never see death?" (v. 48).
5. "Who can deliver his soul from the power of Sheol?" (v. 48).

6. "Where is your steadfast love of old, which by your faithfulness you swore to David?" (v. 49).

All of us can remember times when we sensed the silence of God and wondered if he was really going to keep his promises. All of us can think of times when we felt abandoned and alone. As Christians, we recognize that the unresolved discord of this psalm ultimately points us to the New Testament and to Christ himself. Christ is "great David's greater Son,"[7] and in him the everlasting covenant made to David is fulfilled and made more certain than anything David could have imagined. But we should still allow this psalm to bring us through the agony of this experience. Indeed, even with a limited view of the plan of salvation, the psalmist cries out how God's Anointed One has been mocked (v. 51). The unresolved tensions are finally, and dramatically, met in Christ.

Even though the psalmist cannot see the answer, he is holding on to the hope that God must have some further word which might make sense of the promises of God that he does not yet see fulfilled. Although Psalm 89 ends with the taunts and mocking of the enemies against God's

---

7. James Montgomery, "Hail to the Lord's Anointed," 1821, public domain.

"anointed one" (v. 51 NIV), we must remember that the Hebrew word for the "anointed one" is *messiah* and the Greek word is *Christ*. Psalm 89 brings the third book or collection of the Psalms to a close. It prophetically points to the sober rejection which Jesus Christ bears in his passion. When we are joined in union with Christ as his servants, we, too, may face sober rejection and unresolved pain. This is a crucial part of this journey in better understanding what it means to walk in the path of servanthood. Yet, we are thankful that the sufferings of Christ are neither the last chapter of redemption nor God's final word for us. The hope of the psalmist was not in vain. Even in the darkest point of night, we hope for, and await, the dawn. This is the heart of true servanthood: learning to wait on God's promises even in the midst of our difficulties and pain.

— Chapter Seven —

Christ as Suffering Servant

ISAIAH 50:1–9; 52:13–53:12

In chapters 1 and 2, we highlighted the first two of the Servant Songs of Isaiah. We now come to the last two of these songs, which emphasize Christ as Suffering Servant.

The third Servant Song is found in Isaiah 50:1–9. This song continues the unfolding biography of the Servant, but shifts from an articulation of the final goal to the suffering the Servant will bear in order to fulfill his mission. The song begins by picturing an empty stage upon which no player is present and no voice is heard: "When I came, why was there no one? When I called, why was there no one to answer?" (Isa. 50:2 NIV). Then, in verse 4, the Suffering Servant enters. He has been given "a well-instructed tongue" (v. 4 NIV) and, unlike Israel, he is eager to listen and to obey (vv. 4–5). However, the Servant, like Yahweh, will be rejected. He will be beaten, insulted, and shamed. He will offer his back to those who beat him, his cheeks to those who pull out his beard. He does not turn his head, although they mock him and spit upon his face (v. 6). Quite surprisingly, the Servant willingly accepts this hostility and suffering as part of Yahweh's plan. Because he trusts in Yahweh, the Servant knows that, ultimately, he will be vindicated, his shame lifted, and his disgrace removed (v. 7). The song ends, as it began, with silence. However, this time it is silent because Yahweh has vindicated his Servant and silenced all of his accusers (v. 8). They will all come to nothing, like a garment eaten up by moths (v. 9).

The fourth Servant Song is the one more familiar to Christians because it uses language that has become associated with the cross of Christ in many profound ways. This song is found in Isaiah 52:13–53:12. The preceding context is a picture of a new exodus; Israel is solemnly and triumphantly processing up out of exile. The song opens with a scene in heaven where Yahweh's servant is presented: "See, my servant" (Isa. 52:13a NIV). The Servant is granted a threefold honoring by being "raised and lifted up and highly exalted" (v. 13b NIV). The language reflects the coronation and exaltation of a king, but the Servant is exalted into the very presence of God. However, this extraordinary exaltation is set against the backdrop of suffering. He is "marred" and disfigured (v. 14). He is "despised and rejected by men, a man of sorrows and acquainted with grief" (53:3). It is now explicitly declared that the suffering of the Servant is vicarious: "Surely he has borne our griefs and carried our sorrows" (v. 4). "He was pierced for our transgressions; he was crushed for our iniquities; upon him was the chastisement that brought us peace, and with his wounds we are healed" (v. 5). The song also makes clear that it was the will of Yahweh that his Servant suffer (v. 10), for it was only through the vicarious suffering of the Servant that "my righteous servant will justify many" (v. 11 NIV) and "[bear] the sin of many, [making] intercession for the transgressors" (v. 12).[8] From the outset of this fourth song, the context is before the eyes

---

8. In the Old Testament the concept of vicarious suffering is found in both the sacrificial system as well as the intercession of the prophets on behalf of the people. The Suffering Servant embodies both forms of vicarious suffering.

of not only heaven, but the entire world. The unfolding picture of the Servant is predicted to cause astonishment among the nations, and to silence the kings of the earth (52:15).

There are two dimensions of suffering that I want to highlight in this chapter. We tend to emphasize one of these dimensions, and the other not so much, but both are extremely important for us, especially as we grow in our understanding of servanthood. The first is the Servant suffering for us, or on our behalf. When we think about the sufferings of the Servant, especially as they are fulfilled in Jesus Christ, we quickly, and appropriately, think about the clear message of the New Testament that Christ suffered on the cross on our behalf as a substitutionary atonement for our sins. We link this text and many others to Christ fulfilling the sacrificial system, culminating in Christ as the final sacrifice. This is, of course, a very important theme.

The Substitutionary Suffering of Christ

The book of Hebrews develops this dimension as a central message of that great exposition of the gospel. Hebrews 10, for example, points out several limitations of the Old Testament sacrifice that made it necessary for Christ to come as a final sacrifice. Hebrews extensively develops a type versus fulfillment motif which undergirds the entire book. First, Hebrews points out that the sacrificial system was insufficient because sacrifices had to be offered over and over again, endlessly year after year. If these sacrifices were really efficacious, they could have been offered once and for all. But they had to be repeated. This demonstrates that "it is impossible for the blood of bulls and goats to take away sins" (Heb. 10:4). In other words, the sacrificial system was a temporary provision until Christ came. The sacrifices were like promissory notes that were only validated if Christ came and made them good by affirming that those sacrifices were, in the end, anticipating his final sacrifice for the forgiveness of sins. Thus, sacrifices were a temporary atonement or covering over of sins, but only through Christ are they actually taken away. Sacrifices were the type; Christ was the true fulfillment. This stretches back to Abraham on Mount Moriah. The ram caught in the thicket becomes the type and the later institution of sacrifices was modeled on that—but they were done in anticipation of the later fulfillment.

Second, those who offered the sacrifices were themselves sinners. The Levitical priests first had to offer sacrifices for their own sins, and then for the sins of the people. But Christ (as the true High Priest) is without sin, so not only is the sacrifice better, but the one who offers the sacrifice is a fulfilment of the entire Levitical priesthood. They were the type; Christ was the fulfillment of that type. Hebrews actually says that they serve as "a copy and shadow of the heavenly [realities]" (8:5).

Third, the holy place and the Holy of Holies where these sacrifices were made and offered was designed to be a reflection of heavenly realities. To enter into the Holy of Holies was to enter into the presence of God, but only as an earthly symbol of the actual heavenly presence of God. Christ did enter into the earthly temple, or the earthly Holy of Holies, but actually made substitution for our sins and entered into the very presence of God in heaven, as the ascended, exalted one. Hebrews 9:24 says, "Christ has entered, not into holy places made with hands, which are copies of the true things, but into heaven itself, now to appear in the presence of God on our behalf."

This is a line of thinking that we are all familiar with. The quotation of the Suffering Servant songs in the New Testament makes it clear that the early church understood that Jesus Christ was the Suffering Servant. He was sent on a mission from God that involved suffering on behalf of others. It was only through that suffering that the nations would be redeemed and God's ultimate plan accomplished.

When Jesus came and began to heal the sick and cast out demons, the gospel of Matthew identifies Jesus with the Suffering Servant who "took up our infirmities and bore our diseases" (Matt. 8:17 NIV, quoting Isa. 53:4). Later, after the resurrection, Philip encountered an Ethiopian eunuch in his chariot reading the Suffering Servant Song from Isaiah 53. The book of Acts specifically quotes the passage which says, "Like a sheep he was led to the slaughter and like a lamb before its shearer is silent, so he opens not his mouth" (Acts 8:32, quoting Isa. 53:7). We are told that Philip joined the Ethiopian in the chariot and "beginning with this Scripture he told him the good news about Jesus" (Acts 8:35). The Ethiopian was baptized, becoming not only the first African Christian, but also signifying the global, multiethnic reach of the redemption found in Jesus Christ!

The apostle Peter also identifies the Suffering Servant with Jesus when he declares about Jesus that "He committed no sin, neither was deceit found in his mouth" (1 Peter 2:22, quoting Isa. 53:9). This is why Jesus says in Luke 24:26 to the two on the road to Emmaus, "Was it not necessary that the Christ should suffer these things and enter into his glory?" This is why Peter declares in his sermon on Solomon's Portico after the healing of the lame beggar: "God foretold by the mouth of all the prophets, that his Christ would suffer" (Acts 3:18). This is why Paul preached in the Thessalonican synagogue that the Christ must suffer (Acts 17:3). He makes the same point to King Agrippa and, of course, highlights this repeatedly in his epistles to the early church.

The disciples were totally disillusioned when Jesus was sentenced to die upon the cross. All of their messianic hopes seemed to be dashed to the ground. They did not see how Jesus's death could fulfill all of the kingly, prophetic, and priestly roles which they expected in their long-anticipated messiah. What they did not realize, however, was that there was a deeper plan that they had not anticipated; namely, that God would reveal his greatest glory through suffering. God would be exalted through humiliation. God would ultimately be victorious through suffering defeat. Christ would be both priest *and* sacrifice!

The church, as a whole, has understood this aspect of the sufferings of Christ. It has entered into popular storytelling in many ways. The most obvious one is in C. S. Lewis's well-known story *The Lion, the Witch and the Wardrobe*. The evil witch demands the life of young Edmund who had been revealed as a traitor. She demands exact and unmerciful

Christ as Suffering Servant

payment. What he owes to her must be paid and paid in full. It means nothing less than Edmund's life. The great lion Aslan, who is the Christ-figure in the story, comes forward and tells the evil witch that he will be willing to suffer and die in place of Edmund. The witch agrees and kills Aslan, and celebrates her victory over her archenemy, the lion. However, at the dawn of a new day, Aslan rises from death to life. Aslan explains that although the wicked witch knew the "Deep Magic," which demanded the death of one who is a traitor, her knowledge only goes back to the dawn of time. Aslan knew a "deeper magic from before the dawn of time." That knowledge was that if a willing victim who had committed no treachery offered up his life for the traitor, then death itself would be overturned. This is a picture of what God has done in the gospel of Jesus Christ.

All of the great themes and figures in the Old Testament are brought together and fulfilled through the life and work of the Suffering Servant. Wesley summed up this amazing truth in his hymn, "And Can It Be, That I Should Gain?"

> 'Tis mercy all! Th'Immortal dies!
> Who can explore his strange design?
> In vain the firstborn seraph tries
> To sound the depths of love divine.

> 'Tis mercy all! let earth adore,
> Let angel minds inquire no more!
>
> "He left his Father's throne above,
> So free, so infinite His grace;
> Emptied Himself of all but love,
> And bled for Adam's helpless race;
> 'Tis mercy all, immense and free;
> For, O my God, it found out me.[9]

The mystery of the Suffering Servant is, indeed, a "strange design." Yet, this is what led the apostle Paul to declare that he determined "to know nothing among you except Jesus Christ and him crucified" (1 Cor. 2:2). It is in the presence of the Crucified One, God's Suffering Servant, that we finally begin to see the full contours of God's great plan. In the gift of God's Son into the world—one born to suffer and die—we finally come to fully know and understand the love of God.

---

9. Charles Wesley, "And Can It Be, That I Should Gain?" 1738, public domain.

The Participatory Suffering of the Church

We have explored the first great theme of Christ as Suffering Servant. But there is a second dimension that, as I noted at the outset, is the one we have not emphasized as much. The first theme is that Christ suffers for us. The second theme is that the true servants of the Servant of Yahweh (i.e., the church) share in his suffering. In other words, our theology is not simply that Christ suffers *for* us, but that we suffer *with* him.

The phrase "in Christ" is the classic shorthand for what it means to be in union with Christ. We tend to focus on how we share in his victory and resurrection, and our songs extol this good news, but we sometimes forget that union with Christ also means that we share in his sufferings. In Acts 5 the High Priest and the Sadducees arrested the apostles, questioned them, humiliated them, and beat them before they were released. When they were released, the book of Acts records that they "left the presence of the council, rejoicing that they were counted worthy to suffer dishonor for the name" (Acts 5:41). When Saul of Tarsus was converted on the road to Damascus, the Lord tells Ananias about Paul, "I will show him how much he must suffer for the sake of my name" (Acts 9:16).

This is why Paul declares in Philippians 1:29: "For it has been granted to you that for the sake of Christ you should not only believe in him but also suffer for his sake." Later in the same epistle, Paul tells us that we not only share in the power of his resurrection, but that we are also brought into the fellowship of his sufferings (3:10). Paul tells the church in Colossae that he rejoices in his suffering for their sake, and he even says, quite scandalously, that he "[fills] up what is lacking in Christ's afflictions" (Col. 1:24). Paul tells the church in Thessalonica that "we kept telling you beforehand that we were to suffer affliction" (1 Thess. 3:4). This dimension is all through the New Testament. Paul tells Timothy in his personal correspondence with him that he is to "share in suffering as a good soldier of Christ Jesus" (2 Tim. 2:3).

Bearing the sufferings of Christ is central to what it means to "take up [our] cross" (Matt. 16:24) and carry it into the world. I fear that we have unwittingly declared a gospel that is free from suffering, which is not the gospel of the New Testament. We have been so committed to attraction models of church that we have inadvertently given young Christians a false idea of what it means to follow Christ—a path free from hardship or pain. If someone experiences suffering we interpret it as a kind of "bait

Christ as Suffering Servant

and switch" where God somehow has "not shown up" in our experience the way we were told he would. Many have left the faith because they did not count the cost and they bought into a caricatured version of Christianity that promised prosperity and peace and a life filled with the blessings of God and the glory of Christ, without also realizing that there is no true union with Christ unless we are prepared to suffer with him. We have been told, "In this world you will be blessed because I have overcome the world," whereas Jesus actually said, "In the world you will have tribulation. But take heart; I have overcome the world" (John 16:33). We have been told that the world will love us, whereas Jesus said, "If the world hates you, keep in mind that it hated me first" (15:18 NIV). We have situated ourselves as belonging to this world, whereas Jesus said that we do not belong to this world (17:14). John, the apostle of love, is the one who commanded us at the end of his life to "not love the world or the things in the world . . . For all that is in the world . . . is not from the Father but is from the world" (1 John 2:15–16).

Those of us who belong to the church must accept that being a Christian today in this society involves suffering and rejection. The generation in which we live is hostile to the gospel and they will resist it at every turn, even as we proclaim the glorious good news of what God has done in Jesus Christ. The days of the Christendom truce which allowed for Christianity as long as it accepted a domesticated role in the culture have passed. We thought that Christ alone was that grain of wheat that fell to the ground and died (John 12:24), but it is that very passage that goes on to say that if we love our lives we will lose them, "and whoever hates his life in this world will keep it for eternal life" (v. 25). If we follow Christ, then we can truly be called his servants. To be a servant of Christ is to follow him as the Suffering Servant—the one Isaiah predicted. The prophets of old understood this and were martyred for their message. How much more so will Christ's servants today bear rejection and suffering as we faithfully give witness to him in the world?

― Chapter Eight ―

Servanthood in an Upside-Down Kingdom

MATTHEW 20:20–28

Every year *Forbes* and *Fortune*, two leading business magazines, put out various lists. You would probably have seen from time to time most of the people on these lists as the world's most powerful people and the world's richest billionaires; they even have a list specifying African billionaires. Apparently, Aliko Dangote is the richest African on the continent. Don't forget the eagerly awaited annual list of the Forbes 400, with the four hundred richest people in America (Jeff Bezos, founder of Amazon, tops that list), including the top one hundred richest people in the world. For *Fortune* magazine to name your company as a Fortune 500 company is a big deal. There is the Midas list which gives the top tech investors. This year Alfred Lin won because he had invested heavily in AirBnB and DoorDash food delivery. Other lists put out every year include the people with the most Instagram followers. There are lists of the most famous people based on name recognition around the globe. Hollywood has a so-called "A list" of actors. The lists themselves seem endless. Cristiano Ronaldo has more Facebook followers than anyone else—150 million. Barak Obama, Justin Bieber, and Katy Perry top out the list of the most Twitter followers in the world. I could go on, but my question is this: What do all of these lists tell us about ourselves?

It tells us that we crave fame, recognition, status, and power. This is nothing new. In the ancient world the Roman Empire craved fame, recognition, status, and power as much as anyone. In ancient Rome there were several pathways for this: politics, the military, sports, and public plays. Caesar Augustus was a superstar in his day. Achilles, the hero of the Trojan War and a central character in Homer's *Iliad*, was celebrated as a great military leader. Gladiators and chariot racers in Rome had rabid fan bases that gave them great fame and fortune. Human beings throughout history and around the world crave fame, recognition, status, and power.

The mother of James and John, the sons of Zebedee, wanted her two sons to sit at Jesus's left and right in his kingdom. This request of the mother of James and John must be seen in the way it is presented in Matthew's Gospel; namely, juxtaposed with three times in which Jesus seeks to explain to his disciples what is about to take place. The first time is in Matthew 16 at Caesarea Philippi after the revelation that he is the Messiah: "From that time Jesus began to show his disciples that he must go to Jerusalem and suffer many things from the elders and chief priests and scribes, and be killed, and on the third day be raised" (v. 21). It is here that Peter rebukes Jesus and says, "[No.] This shall never happen to you," and Peter is rebuked (vv. 22–23). The second time is in Matthew after the transfiguration: "The Son of Man is about to be delivered into the hands of men, and they will kill him, and he will be raised on the third day." We are told that the disciples were "distressed" (17:22–23). The third time is just before the passage we are focusing on in this chapter: "The Son of Man will be delivered over to the chief priests and scribes, and they will condemn him to death and deliver him over to the Gentiles to be mocked and flogged and crucified, and he will be raised on the third day" (20:18–19). Notice this third time that the language is heightened with specific mention of mocking and flogging and even the exact manner of his death: crucifixion.

The request for James and John to sit at his right and his left in his kingdom must be understood within this larger setting. Jesus has been telling his disciples what it means to share in his kingdom. This is why Jesus's reply to the mother of the two sons of Zebedee is so apt: "Jesus answered, 'You do not know what you are asking'" (v. 22). They wanted to make it to the top of the *Forbes* list! To sit at a king's right or left hand is a place of honor and prestige. Despite all that Jesus has taught, they still are thinking of his kingdom in a worldly way.

Peter had been rebuked in Matthew 16:23, and in Matthew 19 Peter had told the Lord, "we have left everything and followed you" (v. 27), to which Jesus replied, "many who are first will be last, and the last first" (v. 30). The rebuke of Peter in Matthew 16 and this implied demotion in Matthew 19 meant that perhaps Peter might be going down on the *Forbes* list a notch or two. Every year this happens; Bill Gates is first, then the next year it is Elon Musk, and the following year it is Jeff Bezos. Perhaps the disciples see it like that. Peter has fallen out of favor, so now is the time for James and John to be established as the two on his right and left.

Servanthood in an Upside-Down Kingdom

The kingdom of God is upside down from our normal expectations. The way up is the way down. The only way to Christ is through the cross and through suffering. The indignation of the other ten disciples reveals that they were all in this mode. All of the disciples are vying to get to the top of the *Forbes* list of powerful and influential people. But Jesus calls them all together and reminds them all that the kingdom he is inaugurating is not one of rulership and lording over others like the Gentiles, but the way of servanthood: "whoever would be first among you must be your slave, even as the Son of Man came not to be served but to serve, and to give his life as a ransom for many" (Matt. 20:27–28). The journey of servanthood that we are exploring in this book began with the Suffering Servant of Isaiah, and now we are seeing that it culminates in the cross.

Ben Witherington, a New Testament professor at Asbury Seminary, makes the point that when Jesus says, "the Son of Man came not to be served but to serve, and to give his life as a ransom for many" (v. 28), it is a direct pointer to Isaiah's Servant Songs which Matthew, in particular, has already shown in chapter 12 with his extensive quotation of Isaiah's first Servant Song. These are being fulfilled in Jesus of Nazareth, and if we truly want to be his followers, how much more so should we be servants in the world? If we want to reign with him, we must be willing to suffer with him. The two go together.

The church, yes even the church, is often structured and organized according to power, prestigious appointments, and positions of particular prominence and influence. But Jesus is calling us into an upside-down kingdom where all the worldly values and expectations are being turned on their head. Jesus is the friend of sinners. He is eating with tax collectors and sinners. He allows a redeemed prostitute to anoint him and wipe his feet with her hair. He stands in opposition to both the power structures of Rome as well as the religious power structures of his day and ours.

Jesus says to James and John, "Are you able to drink the cup that I am to drink?" (Matt. 20:22). The cup, of course, is a standard Old Testament image for suffering and wrath. What should boggle your mind is Jesus bringing together into one the two images of "cup" and "kingdom." The way up is the way down. We are now finally coming full circle from the Isaiah Suffering Servant Songs to this: "the Son of Man came not to be served but to serve" (v. 28). If we are to serve Jesus we must enter into his sufferings.

In a few days he would be reigning from a cross. Remember that when Jesus hung on the cross, there were two condemned sinners on either side of him. It is one of the few details of the crucifixion that is found in all four Gospels. It seems that even there, especially there on the cross, Jesus would stand with sinners one last time. He was standing in the place of the condemned with sinners on his right and his left. He even took one more sinner with him from the cross: "today, you will be with me in paradise" (Luke 23:43). Heaven wouldn't be heaven without him, and ten thousand more, because the wedding banquet is drawn not from the powerful, the *Forbes* list, but from the highways and byways. Previously, in chapter 5, we explored the importance of wearing the right wedding clothes to this great banquet of redemption. We pointed out that this refers to the garments of humility, suffering, and servanthood, not the garments of power, influence, and prestige.

There are countless numbers of Christians who will never appear on the *Forbes* lists or the *Fortune* lists or the Midas lists. The church is filled with Sunday school teachers, people who work in homeless shelters, health-care workers, counselors, laborers, shop keepers, among others. None of these are on the list. But we are fundamentally an eschatological people—that is to say, we live out our lives in the present in light of the unfolding future realities that are breaking into this broken world. Sandy Richter has so aptly defined the church as "the outpost of the New Creation in Adam's world." That inherently means that we are living by a different set of standards from those that the world uses to measure life and influence.

This is why Jesus said, "the last will be first, and the first last" (Matt. 20:16). We serve an upside-down kingdom—the way up is the way down! This is why Jesus said, "whoever would be great among you must be your servant" (v. 26). We serve an upside-down kingdom—the way up is the way down! This is why Jesus said about the widow who gave the mite, "She has given more than all the others" (Mark 12:43; Luke 21:3, paraphrased). We serve an upside-down kingdom—the way up is the way down! This is why Jesus said, "Blessed are the poor in spirit, for theirs is the kingdom of heaven" (Matt. 5:3). We serve an upside-down kingdom—the way up is the way down! This is why Jesus said, "Blessed are those who mourn, for they shall be comforted" (v. 4). We serve an upside-down kingdom—the way up is the way down! This is why Jesus said, "The stone that the builders rejected has become the cornerstone" (21:42). We serve an upside-down kingdom—the way up is the way down! This is why one of the earliest Christian hymns found in Philippians 2 says, "though he was in the form of God, did not count equality with God

Servanthood in an Upside-Down Kingdom

a thing to be grasped, but emptied himself, by taking the form of a servant" (vv. 6–7)! We serve an upside-down kingdom—the way up is the way down!

My own discipleship journey will be different from yours, but I want to invite you to think about your own life of being a disciple. Was it men and women who occupied places of power and influence, or humble servants whom God had called to himself? My story begins with my own parents who were, by any accounts, ordinary parents who quietly modeled the faith to us in a thousand ways and pointed us in the direction of the cross. That led me to a point in my junior year of high school to accept an invitation to join a Bible study led by a man named Clyde Fortner. Clyde was a roof contractor, a blue-collar worker who had spent most of his life outside the faith. But in his adult years he had experienced a powerful conversion and eventually led Bible studies in his home. I remember the night he explained the gospel to me and for the first time I really heard it. Right there in his home on a hot July evening in 1976, I invited Jesus Christ into my life by praying the famous Sinner's Prayer. A roof contractor, a servant of Christ, led me to Jesus Christ.

Later, in college I was privileged to come under the teaching of Charles Simpson. Charles was a Baptist minister from the bayous of Louisiana. He was a pastor who had life interrupted by a powerful encounter with the Holy Spirit. This eventually led to his being asked to leave his denomination because his message of the Spirit-filled life was not widely received in his church. But the Lord used him to help me to understand what I now realize was at the heart of the Wesleyan message; namely, that salvation was not just the work of Christ, but the work of the triune God. It was through his ministry that I received the sanctifying work of the Holy Spirit which gave me a redirected heart. In the first half of the gospel, I had been justified, but sin was still my secret lover. As I received the second half of the gospel, I had a heart transformation which empowered me by the Holy Spirit to see the true love of God in ways I had not thought possible. I began to bear fruit as a true disciple and servant of Jesus Christ in the world.

I attended Young Harris, a small two-year Methodist college in Georgia, and graduated in 1979. Then I went to Oral Roberts University, where I met Rev. Bob Stamps, the student chaplain, who took me under his wing and discipled me further. It was under his ministry that I realized that I was being called into full-time Christian service. I was a history major in college, but my life went through another change and I felt led to enroll in seminary to better prepare me to serve Christ in some full-time way.

I went to Gordon-Conwell Theological Seminary, and while many professors had a profound impact on my life, two in particular stand out. The first was J. Christy Wilson Jr. He was born and raised in Iran by missionary parents and early in his life felt a calling to go to Afghanistan as a missionary. He later went and had a fruitful ministry there until he eventually was expelled from the country and ended up at Gordon-Conwell as the professor of missions. Christy Wilson was the most gifted evangelist I have ever met and he introduced the larger world to me. It was through him that I eventually responded to serve Christ in India, which later put me on the track to become a missiologist.

I also was discipled by Gordon Fee, an Assembly of God professor of New Testament at the seminary. Gordon Fee gave me a love for exegesis and for the biblical text which has served as the firm foundation for my entire ministry to the present. Gordon Fee performed the marriage service for my wife, Julie, and me as we entered into a life of ministry together.

Later, I obtained other academic degrees, but these were the most formative years for my discipleship. My point is that Clyde Fortner, Charles Simpson, Bob Stamps, Christy Wilson, and Gordon Fee—those five people had only one thing in common: they were servants of Jesus Christ, and they helped me along the path of servanthood.

Our text links together Christ as the Suffering Servant with all of us who are called into this path of servanthood. In my story, one was a contractor, one was a pastor, one was a chaplain, one was a missionary, and one was an academic. But all five were servants of God.

If you ever go to Tupelo, Mississippi, don't miss visiting the birthplace of Elvis Presley, the King of Rock 'n' Roll. He grew up in a very tiny house. But outside the house they have a very interesting display in the ground which is a big circle of stones with a time line of the life of Elvis Presley. My favorite is the entry for 1946, when Elvis would have been twelve years old. One of his uncles gave him a guitar. You might say, the rest is history. There is no way that his uncle could have anticipated the importance of that formative gift in the life of Elvis Presley. A lot of people give guitars to young boys and girls. But that was a catalytic gift that changed his life.

Some of you will be responsible for running vacation Bible schools, visiting nursing homes, counseling people, preaching sermons, visiting the sick, or cleaning the church. You may not even realize that you are becoming part of this grand unfolding story of redemption into a kingdom of servants.

I was visiting a very sick and elderly man once in early ministry. He didn't attend church regularly, but he was connected to one of the families in our church, so one day I decided to visit him because I heard he was seriously ill and probably wouldn't live long. We chatted together in the kind of normal way people do, but at some point, I asked him if he was ready to meet the Lord face-to-face. He replied that he was not ready, but after more conversation, he let me know that he wanted to come to Jesus. His only request (which might seem odd, but it made sense in the context of this community) was that he didn't want to pray there in his living room to receive Christ. He wanted it to be more "official." He asked if it would be alright if he came forward at the upcoming camp meeting, which was happening not far from his house a few months later. I remember feeling a little hesitant about this plan, but I thought, *Why not?*, so that's what we decided to do.

A few months later I was at this camp meeting—the Loudsville Camp Meeting. This is not one of the nationally known camp meetings that people talk about. Rather, it is just a small local camp meeting for the families in that community. The evangelist preached the gospel and had an altar call. I hadn't told the evangelist that this man would come forward because I wanted to see it for myself, since I wasn't sure if our earlier conversation had taken root. But just as we had planned, he came forward and received the Lord that night under the arbor of a camp meeting.

That night I learned a big lesson about servanthood. I learned that the Great Servant of the kingdom, Jesus Christ, is the only True Evangelist. We are all just privileged to join with him in this great work. It is not about Paul or Apollos (1 Cor. 3:21–23), or about Clyde Fortner or Gordon Fee, or about you or me. It is about Jesus Christ. He alone is the head of this great army of servants who, though derided by the world, transforms the world and ushers in the kingdom like a tiny mustard seed growing under the soil.

→ Chapter Nine ←

A Lesson in Servanthood: A Lion, a King, and a Dead Prophet

1 KINGS 13

One of the early church traditions passed down from Saint John to Polycarp to Irenaeus is the story of John the Apostle sitting in a bathhouse. It is a remarkable story. As Saint John looked around the room, he noticed that sitting across from him was the heretic Cerinthus who was an outspoken Gnostic. Cerinthus argued, for example, that at the return of Christ, our Lord would initiate a one-thousand-year reign of sensual pleasures. Saint John reportedly fled from the bathhouse with his towel wrapped around him for fear that the bathhouse would be struck by the judgment of God. It's one of those moments yet to be captured in Christian art: Saint John with a towel around his waist, fleeing the bathhouse!

In 1 Corinthians 6:18, Paul declares: "Flee from sexual immorality." In addition to fleeing the temptations of the body and the flesh, it is clear that, among other things, we should also flee from heretical and unorthodox versions of Christianity.

It is not a guaranteed experience today to go into a church and hear the gospel faithfully set forth. You will often hear many things in church, mostly tiny narratives which only vaguely connect the man and woman in the pew with the grand story of redemption found in the Scriptures. It is no wonder that so many have left the church. They have been exposed to so much counter-revelation that they scarcely recognize it when the real gospel is actually set forth. The have become so accustomed to all the dribble; the impotent stories; the loss of the prophetic imagination; the domestication of Jesus; the grace of God turned into weak human legalisms; the hostile takeover and hijacking of theology with the language of business, of self-help, of therapeutic self-helpism, of entertainment, and on and on. We can almost say with our Lord Jesus in Luke 10 when he sent out the seventy-two, that

A Lesson in Servanthood: A Lion, a King, and a Dead Prophet

when you go to some churches today, it is like going out "like lambs among wolves" (v. 3 NIV).

Certainly, one of the great imperatives and challenges of any pastor today is to have the courage to get up week after week and faithfully present the gospel of Jesus Christ. Many of you may be in wonderful, godly, faithful churches. But others of you are struggling and you are trying to be faithful in the midst of a difficult situation in your church.

One of the great ways the Scriptures support us in this challenge comes from the Old Testament. As a rule of thumb, the New Testament often teaches directly. Propositions are pronounced, doctrines are exposited, and teaching is given. It is very direct and straightforward. The Old Testament, on the other hand, often functions quite differently. Frequently we encounter the great themes of the Old Testament more indirectly, since much of the content comes not through direct doctrinal teaching, but through stories and narratives. Principles are observed, often without being explicitly stated. Obviously both the New and the Old Testaments teach both directly and indirectly. We do have fairly direct material in the Old Testament, such as the Ten Commandments and important legal passages, but as a rule, the Old Testament prefers to teach indirectly through narrative material.

Likewise, there are important narratives in the New Testament, but the New Testament tends to teach more directly. Indeed, in the wisdom of God's revelation given to us in the Holy Scriptures, many of the great doctrines or themes in the New Testament find their corresponding narrative in the Old Testament which illustrate the same point. It is one thing to hear the doctrine condemning adultery, it is quite another to see the full horror of it lived out in the life of David in his affair with Bathsheba. It is one thing to hear an admonition to obey the voice of the Lord, it is quite another to see the negative consequences of running from God's will in the life of Jonah. It is one thing to be instructed to trust in the Lord, even in difficult situations, it is quite another to read about someone like Abraham or Moses or Gideon who followed the Lord even in difficult situations.

The text focus for this chapter comes from the Old Testament without any commentary or explanations about what is going on. That's the beauty of it. It teaches indirectly, not directly. It is training us in life principles and it does it in a gutsy way. The Old Testament doesn't always model what should happen. It just tells us what happened,

A Lesson in Servanthood: A Lion, a King, and a Dead Prophet

sometimes, tragically unfolded, without footnotes or commentary. It leaves it to us to understand the wisdom that is being taught, even by negation, and to recognize the deeper principles involved. Texts like this can be a great guide and warning if you should ever find yourself in a church situation with some of the same heart-wrenching situations as the prophet from Judah in our text.

First Kings 13 is devoted entirely to the story of a prophet from Judah who is sent to Bethel to announce God's judgment on the house of Jeroboam. It is, by all accounts, considered one of the more difficult passages in the Old Testament so, understandably, there are vast numbers of Christians who have never in their entire lives heard a sermon on this text.

The prophet is called by God to go to Bethel and pronounce judgment on the wicked King Jeroboam who had set up Bethel as a rival site of worship to that which had been established by the word of the Lord. The instruction of God to this unnamed prophet was to travel to Bethel, deliver the word of judgment, and to come home by a different route, neither eating nor drinking anything on the trip.

The prophet obeys. He travels to Bethel, and announces that someday a king named Josiah would come and restore the worship of the true God and burn the bones of the current false prophets, and the sign that this is a true prophecy is that the altar will split open and ashes on it will be poured out.

King Jeroboam immediately pointed to the prophet and cried out, "Seize him" (v. 4). However, immediately the king's hand shriveled and then the altar did, in fact, split open and ashes came out just as the word of the Lord had predicted.

King Jeroboam asks for the prophet to pray for him so that his hand might be restored. The prophet does this and the king's hand is restored. At this point the king realizes that this man is a true prophet of God and so he wants to have fellowship with him and enter into a meal with him. The prophet refuses, recounting the fact that he was commanded to come to Bethel, deliver the prophecy, and return home by a different route without eating or drinking anything.

Now there was an old prophet in Bethel itself who heard about all of this and found out the road on which the prophet went home, and he met him, and invited him to a meal. The prophet at first refused, but when the prophet declared that the Lord had spoken to him and given, as it were, a counter-revelation, the prophet relented and went home and ate with him.

On the way home to Judah, the prophet is killed by a lion. It is a very shocking end to this prophet's life; be maimed by a lion is a clear sign of the judgment of God.

Let's take a moment to do a brief character study of the central characters in the story.

Jeroboam

Jeroboam is the first character in our story to examine. Jeroboam was an impressive leader. In today's world, we would say he had a presence about him—a presence that commanded respect, perhaps even a hint of fear. First Kings 11:28 calls him a "man of standing" (NIV). Solomon was so impressed with his abilities that he put Jeroboam in charge of all his forced labor. Jeroboam was acknowledged by the prophets to be a great leader for Israel. In fact, God appeared to Jeroboam son of Nebat and extended the Davidic promise to him! "If you will listen to all that I command you, and will walk in my ways, and do what is right in my eyes by keeping my statutes and my commandments, as David my servant did, I will be with you and will build you a sure house, as I built for David, and I will give Israel to you" (v. 38). The Lord is saying that if Jeroboam obeyed the Lord and followed after his word, then he would be given a dynasty as enduring as King David.

Jeroboam became king of Israel, but he turned from God and became faithless. If fact, Jeroboam not only turned wholeheartedly to idolatry, he became the enduring symbol of idolatry for all generations. Jeroboam had fled to Egypt during the reign of Solomon, but returned upon Solomon's death. He became the first king of the Northern Kingdom of a divided Israel. Jeroboam became so wicked and so idolatrous that he became the standard for unfaithfulness to the covenant, the shorthand for a wicked, unbelieving heart, and the epitome of what it meant to forsake the living God. The phrase "the sins of Jeroboam" became a constant refrain for the kings of Israel (1 Kings 14:16; 15:26, 30; 16:2, 19, 26, 31; 2 Kings 10:29, 31; 13:2, 6, 11; 14:24; 15:9, 18, 24, 28; 17:22). Jeroboam represents a counterclaim of revelation that is absolutely clear. God's covenant said "*this*" and Jeroboam said, "No, we're going to do *that*."

Jeroboam, for me, represents in our own day, a symbol of what it means to embody a post-Christendom world. If you had lived in the time between the death of Solomon and the eventual deportation by the Assyrians into exile in 722 BC, you would have lived in what would have felt like

A Lesson in Servanthood: A Lion, a King, and a Dead Prophet

the period we are in now. The heyday of covenantal faithfulness was clearly in their rearview mirror. Like us, they may have overly romanticized the Davidic or Solomonic period, but even allowing for this, they knew that there were all kinds of lines that had been crossed.

Jeroboam, for starters, decided to set up his own priesthood. He would appoint priests, regardless of what tribe they were from. Jeroboam then set up all kinds of idols. Eventually, Asherah poles and altars to Baal and shrines under every spreading tree became commonplace in the Northern Kingdom. This is the legacy of Jeroboam son of Nebat.

I would suspect that most of you understand this, and you are on your guard against the spirit of Jeroboam in our own day. Jeroboam is the whole sociopolitical force that seeks to set up a rival system to counter the revelation of God. The intent is to tear down any sense of the eternal and any reliance upon divine revelation in the Bible, and construct a wholly godless society where everyone does what is right in their own eyes. That is the sin of Jeroboam son of Nebat. In fact, if you read all of the one hundred references to Jeroboam in the Scripture, his sin is more than just setting up alternative idolatrous worship sites. It is deeper than that. It is his whole rejection of the revelation of God and supplanting it with his own counter-revelation.

The collapse of confidence in the Christian metanarrative in our culture has to be seen against the backdrop of the construction of a counter-revelation which asserts that we are at the center of human history. We sometimes fail to see that the world is deeply committed to its own catechesis. Young men and women are trained from birth to assert their own independence against God. It happens in a thousand small ways. Jeroboam represents the idolatrous counternarrative of this world.

Old Prophet

The next character we will look at is the old prophet who we meet at the end of the story. We don't even know the name of the old prophet from Bethel, but oh how the spirit of this prophet continues until the present day. This old prophet lived in Bethel. Since the idolatry of Jeroboam was centered in Bethel, you should note that God sent for a prophet from Judah to come up to Bethel. This old prophet was not reliable. He was a retired prophet. Now, some men and women of God, upon retirement, go even deeper with the Lord, spend more time in prayer, and finally feel free

A Lesson in Servanthood: A Lion, a King, and a Dead Prophet

to give of their time to the needy in ways which seemed impossible during their normal work life. But I have seen other tragic examples of laypeople and even pastors who have served faithfully who, in retirement, go off the rails and fight against the very faith they once defended. This prophet represents the decaying hulk of human religion gone stale.

The old prophet once had a call from God. His calling was not in the political realm, but he was sent to uphold the prophetic word in the midst of the people of God. He seems to represent the fading shell of the prophetic office. He retained the name and the title and the position, but somewhere along the way he had lost the true spirit of a man of God.

This may be the man or woman who still retains their office in the church. There are pastors of churches and professors in university divinity schools and even seminaries who have been given the stewardship of the Word of God, but have long forsaken its truth and its power. To use the language of the New Testament, they are "having a form of godliness but denying its power" (2 Tim. 3:5 NIV). This is one of the hardest forces to face because we are prepared to defend the gospel against external attacks and derision, but we are often caught off-guard when those attacks come from within the church itself, especially when it comes from the lips of clergy.

Man of God from Judah

The man of God from Judah is the next character in the story. He successfully resisted the overt call from Jeroboam to join in the rebellion and forsake the Lord and unite with the counter-revelation. However, he was not as successful in understanding that the greatest danger sometimes is within our own movement: the people of God. It was Lesslie Newbigin who reminded us that it was the people of God who crucified the Lord Jesus Christ. The old prophet in Bethel knew the Word of God, but was prepared, in effect, to slay the prophet of God, by enticing him into sharing a meal in direct opposition to the command of God.

This year, if you are a United Methodist, you will be acutely aware of the disruptions taking place to derail the ministries of those who are committed to a high Christology and the authority of Scripture—and it is coming from within the church itself. Even if you are in another denomination, this is something you may have experienced. The man of God from Judah made a fateful assumption that the old prophet must be a man of God—and it cost him his life.

Lion

If you read the text quickly you may think that the story is limited to these main characters—Jeroboam, the man of God from Judah, and the old prophet from Bethel, all interacting over their vision for the future of the people of God in the Northern Kingdom. But there are actually four characters in the story, not just three. There is this lion. The donkey is also there, but to accentuate the lion.

Amazingly, the lion kills the prophet and then stands quietly by. He doesn't further mangle the dead body, nor does he attack the donkey. He just stands there. He is the only figure in the narrative who actually obeys the command of the Lord. He exercises God's judgment and then stands in obedience. He exercises the Lord's command and nothing more—not adding to it or taking anything away.

Ironically, the lion in the text represents covenant faithfulness. It is a terrifying thing to fall into the hands of the living God. There is nothing that should terrify you more than to have the truth of God, without the truth of God having you!

The Life of Servanthood

Servanthood is standing ready and prepared to do the Master's bidding, neither adding to nor taking away from the word of the Lord. The lion is the only real hero of the story. The political apparatus had become corrupt. The religious life in the Northern Kingdom had become swallowed up in the surrounding political corruption. Even the prophet of God from Judah ended up becoming a victim to the tragedy of the North. But the lion is the only one standing when the text is over.

Later, the old prophet comes up to recover the body of the man from Judah. The lion is still standing there. He hasn't mangled the body. He hasn't attacked the donkey. The donkey is also still standing there. The old prophet takes the body, puts it on the donkey, and brings it back to Bethel. The man from Judah is honored in his death as a true prophet, but his ministry has been tragically cut short.

Every pastor or church leader with wonderful ministries must never forget that they will be tested at several critical moments. It is so important that you remember this prophet from Judah, and that you not let your ministry be cut unnecessarily short. The servant is the one who stands ready to do what the Master said to do. He or she is not swayed by the world. The culture will scream at you. The institutional church has its wily ways to entice you to

A Lesson in Servanthood: A Lion, a King, and a Dead Prophet

accept false doctrines. But the true servant of God stands firm. This is the lesson of servanthood: learning to stand firm in the midst of whatever comes your way in order to distract you from God's eternal word and calling.

The apostle John had apparently read the tragic story of 1 Kings 13. As he sat in the bathhouse in Rome, he realized that he didn't want to have his ministry cut short. So he thought, "What should the prophet from Judah have done after he had delivered his powerful prophecy against Jeroboam?" He had been told to go up and deliver the message and then get back as quickly as possible. Don't eat or drink anything. Just go and come back as fast as you can. So John got up, rebuked Cerinthus, and ran out of the bathhouse as fast as he could with nothing but a towel on. Now that is a picture of servanthood!

Epilogue

We have been on a journey together learning more about servanthood. We have endeavored to understand the marks of a distinctively Christian vision of servanthood. The journey began by recognizing that we cannot even begin to comprehend or live out servanthood until we first acknowledge that it all flows from *the* Servant—the Servant of God, Jesus Christ. He is the pattern and archetype and embodiment of all servanthood.

This journey has also helped us to recognize that God's redemptive plan is for all nations to come to himself. That means that we must serve Christ until men and women from every tribe, every nation, and every language call upon him, in fulfillment of that great vision of the apostle John (Rev. 7:9–10). God set this plan in motion from the days of Abraham and through the prophets and amazing history of Israel, but it reaches its climax in the incarnation of God in Jesus Christ.

Jesus Christ came as the great fulfillment of the Servant of God. We are called into union with him. As we are conformed to his likeness, we become people of great hope and vision, like Hannah and Mary. We become people of obedience who hear God's voice and do it, just as the Servant of Yahweh did in Isaiah's prophecies, which became fully realized in Jesus Christ. That is the great call to which we are all seeking to respond to. As his servants, this is a call to not only the blessed joys of reconciliation and forgiveness, but also to follow him in the path of suffering for the sake of a lost world. We become fellow sufferers bearing in our bodies the scorn of the world and willingly sharing in Christ's suffering.

You may not be in a position of full-time ministry in the formal sense as an ordained minister of the gospel, but the great work of redeeming the world involves every one of us. We all must become servants of faithfulness who hold fast to the Word of God and are not deceived by or consumed by the cultural and church storms that rage around us. Each person reading these pages has an important work in discipling others and learning to lean into the life of Christ in the day-to-day work and life to which he

Epilogue

has called us. We all have opportunities to obey him and to serve him in the places and among the people he has placed us. It is my deepest prayer that you will discover that place in a fresh way in the days and months ahead. For we are all servants of God, serving the great Servant of God, Jesus Christ, co-laborers with him for the redemption of the world.

Printed by Libri Plureos GmbH in Hamburg, Germany